Proximity

Evangelism the Natural Way

Eric Kuykendall

ISBN 978-0-578-19576-6

Printed in USA by 48HrBooks

Dedication

To the men and women who modeled for me evangelism. Thank you Dr. Wilton for always putting evangelism at the very center of all of your pursuits. Thank you Sal Barone for living out a daily pursuit of leading people to Jesus.

Thank you Kylie for pushing me beyond my perceived limitations and into the world of risk. Who else would tell me to walk unannounced into a Buddhist temple in Croft just for the chance to engage the lost?

Thank you First Baptist Spartanburg for taking a chance. In a world that has lost its evangelistic fervor, you are forging a new frontier in this increasingly apathetic culture. God bless you as you follow the Lord and His Great Commission.

Table of Contents

Introduction

God must have a sense of humor. I am the last person who should be writing a book about evangelism. I am not comfortable with any stage of this process. Butterflies still dance around in my stomach. Fear still blankets my mind. I worry about offending or saying the wrong thing at the wrong time. Who am I to write a book on evangelism when there are others who do it so naturally?

God gave some the gift of evangelism. I think of my friend Sal Barone who absolutely relishes every opportunity to bring up the good news of Jesus to anyone who will listen. Actually, he will bring up the gospel whether they listen or not! He has the spiritual gift of evangelism. I find it very hard to relate to him because my spiritual giftings are different.

Whereas I might be an unusual choice for an author on this subject, I hope that this book will be relatable. If you do not have the gift of evangelism, you are like me and need to find a way to still make this Christian duty a part of your life. We do not get a pass on evangelism just because it does not come easy.

This book is for those of us who need help with sharing the gospel. God has given me a method that I believe can be adopted into your life as a natural way of evangelizing. It involves opening your life up to lost people and being in proximity to them. Evangelism then becomes a natural extension of your love and compassion for them.

Your life will change when you begin to focus on evangelism. You will see God move like never before. You will experience some of the greatest joys in life and be drawn to deeper prayer. May the Lord bless you in so many ways as you seek to bring your friends, neighbors, coworkers, and family one step closer to Jesus!

Chapter One
From Ambivalence to Ambassador

I had a precarious introduction to evangelism. I was about six years old when my mom and I first visited the First Baptist Church of Corpus Christi, Texas. Late that day after a fun afternoon of playing, my mom suddenly scampered through the house and turned off all the lights. She ran to the living room where I was watching television and quickly turned off my show.

"Hey! What are you doing Mom? I was watching that!"

She looked at me with those no-nonsense eyes and put her finger to her lips. Suddenly the doorbell rang and my mom grabbed my arm, holding me down. My heart started racing with both fear and excitement.

"Just be very quiet," my mom whispered as the doorbell rang a second time. Were we spies that had been outed? Was my mom on the run against the law? My mind raced as these persistent visitors knocked on the door.

After a certain amount of time had passed, my mom released her death grip on my arm. "What is going on?" I asked with a new sense of excitement that my life had suddenly turned into an action movie.

"Those were some folks from the church we visited. I didn't want them to know we were home." Mom peeked through the window blinds then went back to what she was doing.

I laugh about that now because it would be just seventeen years later that I would be ringing the doorbell at the home of a church visitor as I anxiously anticipated sharing the gospel. Life has a funny way of coming full circle.

Do you remember the first time you encountered someone coming to share the gospel with you or your family?

_____

_____

The word "evangelism" can evoke a variety of thoughts and emotions. In an informal survey, I asked participants to give me the first couple of words that came to mind when I say the word "evangelism". Some of the responses were:

- Hard work
- Getting real
- Revival
- Preaching
- Missionary work
- Witness
- Risk
- Youth missions
- Visitation
- Going out in groups and knocking on doors

What comes to your mind when you hear the word "evangelism?"

_____

_____

For many people it is the scary "E word." The very thought of sharing the gospel with another person brings shivers. Others believe evangelism is the work of the preacher and missionaries. Still others equate evangelism with revivals or church outreach programs.

Evangelism ought to bring some sense of fear or reverence because it is a matter of eternal significance. But evangelism is certainly not meant to be relegated to the preacher, to missionaries, or to an outreach program. Rather, evangelism is the work of *every* believer to proclaim the good news of the death, burial, and resurrection of Jesus Christ.

Rather, evangelism is the work of every believer to proclaim the good news of the death, burial, and resurrection of Jesus Christ.

8

Evangelism is the Work of All Believers

The Bible is absolutely clear on this issue. Evangelism is the work of all believers. Dr. Don Wilton is known for his evangelistic zeal throughout the world. His pulpit ministry at First Baptist Spartanburg and the many revivals he has led over forty years of gospel ministry has accounted for thousands of salvations. But his church cannot rely upon his preaching to do all the evangelism. God did not call Dr. Wilton to carry that load by himself. God has called the members of First Baptist Spartanburg to be the primary ambassadors for Christ in Spartanburg County.

The Apostle Paul said to the Corinthian believers:

[18] *All this is from God, who through Christ reconciled us to himself and gave us the ministry of reconciliation;* [19] *that is, in Christ God was reconciling the world to himself, not counting their trespasses against them, and entrusting to us the message of reconciliation.* [20] *Therefore, we are ambassadors for Christ, God making his appeal through us. We implore you on behalf of Christ, be reconciled to God.* (2 Corinthians 5:18-20)

We as believers have been entrusted with the message of reconciliation. This message is known as the gospel. It is the story of how God rescued a hopelessly corrupt people from their eternal destination of hell and offered His only begotten Son, perfectly sinless, as a substitute so that those who believe will be reconciled to God. That is our message to proclaim.

We are called ambassadors for Christ.

Recently former South Carolina Governor Nikki Haley was appointed the United States Ambassador to the United Nations. What is her function as an ambassador? How is that similar to our role as an ambassador for Christ?

_____

_____

_____

In the time of the New Testament, an ambassador involved three roles:

    (1) a commissioning for a special assignment

    (2) representing the sender

    (3) exercising the authority of the sender[i]

As believers today we have been commissioned by Jesus to go and "make disciples of all nations, baptizing them in the name of the Father and of the Son and of the Holy Spirit" (Matthew 28:19). That is our Great Commission. God has commissioned us as believers to go into the world and preach the gospel.

You might say, "I don't feel qualified to go out and preach the gospel. My past is too shady. I struggle to follow all the commands of Christ." Welcome to the club! We all feel that way. God is not looking for a qualified person. He's looking for an available person. Greg Laurie says, "God is not looking for ability as much as He is looking for availability. God does not call the qualified; He qualifies the called."[ii]

> God is not looking for a qualified person. He's looking for an available person.

As ambassadors for Christ we represent the sender. In the Great Commission we have the familiar word "go." A strict translation of the original language shows the Greek word for "go" is literally translated "going" or "as you go". The implication is that the process of making disciples – including the initial sharing of the gospel to them – happens "as you go." Evangelism is a lifestyle where we represent the sender, Jesus, wherever we go. So many believers are not actively pursuing this commission. As a result many churches have become stagnate and are closing down. Interestingly the churches reaching the most people for the gospel are the newest churches that launch with an evangelistic zeal. But the age of a church should never be a prerequisite for enthusiasm.

Finally the ambassador exercises the authority of the sender. Again we go to the Great Commission which begins: "All authority in heaven and on earth has been given to me" (Matthew 28:18). By the authority vested in Jesus, His ambassadors are commissioned to go out into the world and tell the world about Jesus. We are not given the authority to rule – much like the Roman ambassadors were not given that authority from the king. But we are given the authority to proclaim the sacred message of reconciliation to a lost and dying world.

Who has been an ambassador for Christ to you? What characteristics did they exhibit that made you think of Christ? Are you an active ambassador for Jesus?

_____

_____

_____

Evangelism is Hard. Why Should I Do This?

There is a legitimate reason why so many people are not actively pursuing their friends, family members, neighbors, and co-workers for Christ. Evangelism is hard. Many believers feel completely inadequate for the job because they have not been trained and have never seen anyone model evangelism. Fear grips the heart of many believers because each evangelistic effort involves risk. "What if doing this costs me my friend?" "They might ask me questions I can't answer." "They might reject what I say!" These fears are probably more perceived than real, but perception matters.

While evangelism may be hard, we are given biblical reasons why we need to do this hard thing. Below are three primary reasons why we need to overcome our fears and pursue the lost for Christ. Which of the reasons below is most compelling to you?

God did not spare His own Son.

Evangelism is important because God did not spare His own Son. The message of the gospel is not just "okay" news. We are not offering up a self-improvement plan. The gospel is not just one of many options to help a person get centered in their life. No, the gospel is radical in its very nature.

[God] did not spare his own Son but gave him up for us all (Romans 8:32)

For God so loved the world, that he gave his only Son, that whoever believes in him should not perish but have eternal life. (John 3:16)

but God shows his love for us in that while we were still sinners, Christ died for us. (Romans 5:8)

The message of the gospel says that a Jewish court and the Roman authorities declared Jesus guilty and unrighteous. He was spit on, slapped, and mocked. He was sent to His death as a condemned man. Then we - the true guilty party - are declared not guilty and righteous.

If God went to these great lengths to bring us reconciliation to Himself, do you think that evangelism is important to Him? Do you realize that this message contains the most outrageous, unfathomable act of love ever conceived and it temporarily cost God His Son? What would God think of us keeping this message to ourselves out of fear of offending?

In the fall of 2016, the quarterback for the San Francisco 49ers, Colin Kaepernick, refused to stand during the national anthem. Millions of Americans were enraged because they viewed the flag as symbolic for freedom, which was bought with the precious blood of good men and women. Most Americans proudly fly the American flag, sing the national anthem, and boast of the greatness of our country. Does your love and zeal for America pale in comparison to your love and zeal for the gospel? They both are bought with blood. But only one kingdom matters for eternity. Believers are, first and foremost, citizens of the Kingdom of God. God did not spare His own Son. The world will know that act of love was significant when we make personal evangelism a top priority in life.

Why does Jesus' death and resurrection make evangelism important?

_____

_____

_____

You were once a fish.

While Peter and Andrew were busy casting their nets into the sea, Jesus came upon them and said, "Follow me, and I will make you fishers of men" (Matthew 5:19). While we typically think of that passage as Jesus' call to his followers to reach the lost, let us not forget that we all were once a fish.

The sea of life is brimming with fish that need to be caught. You were once in that sea, aimlessly swimming, lacking purpose, and a prisoner of the deep. The second chapter of the book of Ephesians gives a spiritual definition of a "fish"

- Dead in sin (vs 1)
- Follower of the ways of this world (vs 2)
- Being led by the whispers of Satan (vs 2)
- Dominated by the desires of the flesh (vs 3)
- Separated from Christ (vs 12)
- Without hope (vs 12)

That was once a description of you. Do you remember how far you have come? Incidentally that also accurately described Martin Luther, Dwight L. Moody, Billy Graham, and William Carey. Who was the Sunday School teacher that led Dwight L. Moody to Christ? Who was the elderly woman who prayed religiously for twenty years that Billy Graham would come to faith in Christ? Had it not been for these "fishers of men," the 19th century of American church history would have looked much different.

Your compulsion to share the gospel will increase in direct proportion to your recognition of God's grace in your life. In the graph below you will see that your compulsion to share the Good News of Jesus Christ grows as your awareness of God's grace and how far you have come since you were a "fish" increases.

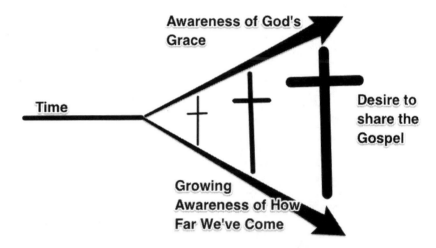

All around you are fish that are in utter darkness without Christ. Many of them are struggling significantly with their addiction to gratify the lusts of the flesh. Others appear to be good, decent people, but they are at "enmity with God" (Romans 8:7 NKJV). You were just like them at one time. The Bible puts it this way:

And such were some of you. But you were washed, you were sanctified, you were justified in the name of the Lord Jesus Christ and by the Spirit of our God. (1 Corinthians 6:11)

But God, because of His great love for you, appointed an ambassador to cast a net. A faithful fisherman caught you. Now you are "alive together with Christ—by grace you have been saved" (Ephesians 2:5) and God "raised [you] up with him and seated [you] with him in the heavenly places in Christ Jesus" (Ephesians 2:6). Are you motivated yet? Why would our past as a lost "fish" motivate us to share the gospel?

_____

_____

`

_____

Staying Silent About the Gospel is Sin

The Great Commission is not the Great Suggestion. Research shows that ninety-five percent of all American Christians have never led a person to faith in Christ.[iii] The Great Commission has become the Great Omission.

The uncomfortable truth is that staying silent about the gospel is sin. We have been given clear marching orders from our Lord.

- "Go therefore and make disciples..." (Matthew 28:19)
- "You will be my witnesses..." Acts 1:8
- "For so the Lord has commanded us, saying, 'I have made you a light for the Gentiles, that you may bring salvation to the ends of the earth.'" (Acts 13:47)
- "Go into all the world and proclaim the gospel to the whole creation." (Mark 16:15)
- "And the gospel must first be proclaimed to all nations" (Mark 13:10)

When we do not participate in the active proclamation of the gospel, we are guilty of the sin of omission. A sin of omission is not doing what you know you should. The Bible says,

> When we do not participate in the active proclamation of the gospel, we are guilty of the sin of omission.

So whoever knows the right thing to do and fails to do it, for him it is sin. (James 4:17)

In some states, failure to report a crime you have witnessed is itself a crime. Under Texas law, for example, you can be charged with a Class A misdemeanor for failing to report an offense that resulted in serious

15

bodily injury or death. If you came across a building on fire and saw a person in the window, I would hope that you would quickly help in whatever way you can. To do nothing would be downright criminal!

Yet we have people in our inner circle of friends, family, and neighbors obliviously going about their day while the building they are in is on fire. Are we going to quietly pretend this is not happening? Are we going to talk to them about sports, restaurants, and politics while the clock is ticking toward eternity?

The last thing God wants is for them to choose eternal separation from Him. The Lord is "not wishing that any should perish, but that all should reach repentance" (2 Peter 3:9). That is why He sent Jesus to live a perfect life, die on the cross for our sins, and rise from the dead. God wants you to be His ambassador and be His chosen instrument for their rescue. He is searching for someone who will say, "Use me, Lord!" Would you be that person?

Next Step

Conviction does not equal obedience. It is time for you to start obeying. Begin by creating a "Name List." This is a short list of names of people that you suspect do not know Jesus as their Lord and Savior. These names should come from your circle of relationships including your family, friends, neighbors, and co-workers. Pray "God bring to mind people in my inner circle who do not follow Jesus."

Name List

_____

_____

_____

_____

_____

Now start praying for these names. Do no procrastinate. Do it now. Pray that God will open up the hearts of these people in the coming days as you prepare to be their ambassador for Christ. May God use YOU to bring one of these to faith. In Jesus name I pray, AMEN!!

Chapter Two
Anyone, Anywhere, and Any Time

Christians tend to spend most of their time with other Christians. As the old saying goes, "Birds of a feather flock together." This should not come as a surprise. Human beings favor those who are similar to them on a wide rang of categories. Whereas family and kinship are the most powerful source, people also seek out those who have similar tastes in political views, religion, sports team loyalty, music preference, body type, and socioeconomic order.[iv]

Christians who derive their values from the Bible and actively follow Jesus will often congregate together both on Sunday mornings and throughout the week. As the years go by, Christians will trend toward isolating themselves from a culture that stands in sharp contrast to their principles. The net result is a lack of evangelism because so many Christians do not have an unbeliever in their inner circle of acquaintances.

As one who works at a church and is surrounded by Christians up and down my street, I wrestled with the reality that I did not have an active relationship with a lost person. My "Name List" was barren. I decided to do something about it.

I knew I was going to coach my son's baseball team in the spring. My inclination was to ask my good friend from church to coach the team with me. But I knew of a guy – the father of my son's best friend - that could also coach. He was far from God and I was burdened for him and his son. So I asked him to be my assistant coach.

Throughout the season I used small opportunities to transition the conversation to spiritual matters. Those conversations led to invitations to church. Finally, on Easter morning, he came to church and responded during the invitation.

I would not have had the joy to see this decision had I not made the conscious effort to be intentional about evangelism. Are you like me? Do you have a limited inner circle of people who are lost? **Fill out the following chart to analyze your inner circle.**

Family	Neighbors	Co-Workers	Friends

Fill in your 5 closest relationships in each category

Mark each: ✚ Saved, ✖ Lost, ? Don't Know

Circle 3 of the ✖'s and the ?'s and put them on your Name List

19

Evangelism is limitless in time, place, or person. Even in the most restricted nations, the Christian is called to reach anyone, anywhere, and at any time. How much more should we take advantage of living in a country that allows us to freely share our faith to whomever, wherever, and whenever we want?

Anyone

According to the website "Bible Gateway," the most popular verse in the entire Bible is John 3:16. Many Christians know this verse well because it was their first memorized verse. The King James Version renders the words this way:

For God so loved the world, that he gave his only begotten Son, that whosoever believeth in him should not perish, but have everlasting life.

The gospel is for "whosoever." This is such an important word. It means anyone; no one is excluded. It is universal, global, and without borders. It knows no socioeconomic order. The gospel is as much for the blond-haired, blue-eyed seven-year-old boy as the thirty-year-old tattoo artist with a drug addiction. "Whosoever" includes your boss at work and the barista you see every week at the local coffee bar. The gospel is for that far-left social justice warrior and the Hindu working in the cubicle across the office. God's love and compassion goes out to all.

Ultimately you want to share with everyone because you never know whom God will choose. God loves everyone and wants all people to hear the Good News. In the Parable of the Sower, the sower "went out to sow" (Matthew 13:3). The seed fell along a path, on rocky ground, among thorns, and in good soil. In the end only the good soil produced grain that lasted. But the sower did not discriminate. He put the seed out everywhere and was prepared for a crop. Sowing the seed of the gospel is our responsibility. Only the Holy Spirit can make the seeds grow. So we share with anyone because Jesus said "whosoever."

But while evangelism is meant for you to apply to anyone, we know that we cannot share the gospel with everyone we come in contact with. Otherwise we would be sharing the gospel multiple times every day. While that concept sounds great, that is also not realistic. Jesus did not model that for us. Rather, Jesus gave his followers a different approach. We need to pursue the "low-hanging fruit."

My stepfather has a delightful garden at his ranch filled with a variety of fruits and vegetables. Every year my children get to spend thirty minutes walking through the rows of plants and pick certain fruits and vegetables. Since they are young and relatively new at the science of picking fruit, they will pick the most accessible ones they can find. These are the low-hanging fruit.

As it relates to evangelism, many of us are like children. We do not have much experience with sharing the gospel. Therefore we need to go after the "low-hanging fruit." These are the people in our lives that have shown an interest in spiritual matters. Perhaps they grew up in a church-going household but have not attended consistently in years. They are the people in your life that you have established a level of trust. These people will call or email you when they have a need for prayer or comfort. These are our family members, our neighbors, our friends at school, our co-workers, and those with whom we socialize on a regular basis.

God may call you to reach that hardcore atheist that spews hatred toward Christians. But do not forget about the friend who is suffering and needs to hear about a Savior that suffered in our place.

The chart at the beginning of this chapter probably has the names of some low-hanging fruit. Circle the names of two or three that are the most accessible for the gospel. What specifically makes these people the most ready for a gospel conversation?

_____

_____

_____

Anywhere

As mentioned in the first chapter, the Great Commission gives us the command to "go." However a more literal translation of the Greek word *poreuthentes* is "going" or "as you are going." The major implication for all Christians is that individual believers primarily share their faith as they go about their normal daily activities.

Believers should not view evangelism as a program of the church – though the church is certainly right to organize evangelistic programs. Believers should not view evangelism as the job of the preacher – though he should lead the way in example. Rather, evangelism is the work of *every* believer to proclaim the good news of Jesus Christ anywhere they go.

Make sure you do not pigeonhole evangelism as something that always looks like a person with a New Testament in their hand and asking everyone "What do you understand it takes for a person to go to Heaven." Evangelism is like a Christian on a mission. Author Michael Frost says, "Evangelistic mission works effectively when we are living generous, hospitable, Spirit-led, Christlike lives as missionaries to our own neighborhoods."[v] The Apostle Paul put it this way, "Walk in wisdom toward outsiders, making the best use of the time. Let your speech always be gracious, seasoned with salt, so that you may know how you ought to answer each person" (Colossians 4:5-6).

An excellent form of evangelism is to live what Frost calls "questionable lives." These are the kind of lives that evoke questions from neighbors, friends, co-workers, and family members. While we will investigate this more in the next chapter, the point is that believers must participate in the lives of the unbelievers in their inner circle of acquaintances. You must leave your "Christian bubble."

A good fisherman does not indiscriminately toss his lure into the water. He intentionally heads toward the places where he thinks the fish will be congregating. Believers are called to be "fishers of men" (Mark 1:17). Believers are fishermen and ought to intentionally go to the fishing holes that have the swarms of fish.

Are you taking the gospel with you wherever you go? Where are some places you can target as "fishing holes" in your life?

_____

_____

_____

Any Time

Church leaders have worked tirelessly to keep evangelism a priority for church members. They have created programs to help facilitate the work of sharing the gospel. While these programs have been very fruitful and effective, the unintentional consequence has been the compartmentalization of sharing the gospel. Many Christians have unintentionally relegated the work of evangelism to the times when the church calls on them to share their faith – whether that be revivals, visiting nights, or special outreaches. When should Christians share their faith? The short answer is whenever!

Paul said to his mentee Timothy "be ready in season and out of season" (2 Timothy 4:2). Another translation puts it, "Be ready to spread the word whether or not the time is right."[vi]

The command is to "be ready." In the previous chapter of 2 Timothy, Paul calls upon Timothy to be a "good soldier" (2 Timothy 3:4). I have never been a soldier or engaged in combat, but I can imagine a soldier is extremely alert during a battle. His ears can hear a twig snap. His eyes work overtime to focus on the smallest detail. His hands and fingers are ready to react on a split second. Like a good soldier, Timothy (and us) was to always be at his post, and alert to embrace every opportunity of making known the gospel.

Possibly the most important way to "be ready" is to pray about opportunities to witness. As the old adage goes, "if you pray for rain, bring an umbrella." God loves to put unbelievers in the path of Christians who ask for the opportunity to reach out to them. Praying for the opportunity to reach specific people today will sharpen your senses, stimulate your awareness, and heighten your expectation. Pray a prayer like this:

> Possibly the most important way to "be ready" is to pray about opportunities to witness.

Lord, prepare opportunities in my path today to have gospel conversations. Give me the words to say and the manner in which to say them during someone else's time of need. Prepare their hearts to be receptive to the good news you want me to share. Make me ready. Make me willing. In Jesus' name I pray, Amen.

It is interesting that Paul uses the phrase "in season and out of season." What does he mean here? Is there a "witnessing season" much like there is a "hunting season?"

Bible scholars differ over exactly how to translate the phrase Paul uses. What impression do you get of Paul's intention from the following translations?

- even if it isn't the popular thing to do (CEV)
- whether the opportunity seems to be favorable or unfavorable. [Whether it is convenient or inconvenient, whether it is welcome or unwelcome (Amp)
- whether it is convenient or inconvenient (NAB)
- welcome or unwelcome (NJB)
- whether the time is favorable or not (NLT)
- favorable or unfavorable (NRSV)

There are times in your life when you are filled with the Spirit, feeling very generous, and sensitive to the lost. Those are "in season" times. There are other times when you do not want to think about anyone other than yourself. You have had a bad day, a bad week, or a bad month when nothing seems to go your way. Those are "out of season" times. Christians need to be ready to share the gospel in season *and* out of season because you never know how God is going to use your circumstances to build a bridge for their salvation.

One of my greatest mentors was a man named Mike Fechner. I worked for Mike as an intern during my first year serving in the local church. Mike was a dreamer and a visionary. Aside from being the Minister of Education at one of the largest churches in America, Mike founded H.I.S. BridgeBuilders – an urban missionary organization that breaks the cycle of poverty by confronting the spiritual needs of the poor.[vii] While I was working with Mike, he was "in season." He was aware of the lost around him. He was sensitive to spiritual needs. And he was ready to share the gospel at any given opportunity.

Nowhere in his plan did stage four lung cancer exist. This was a man that would work tirelessly to equip the saints at his megachurch and then alleviate poverty in the poorest regions of Dallas. Now he would be drained of his energy as he walked though chemo wards with an IV bag.

This should have been an "off season" for him to focus on his health and recovery. But his suffering gave him a special heart for all the other cancer patients lying in their rooms. He grabbed his IV pole, walked around, and chatted with everyone. He made his rounds to patients, their families, the nurses, and doctors. After visiting with them for a while, he would ask how he could pray for them. Soon "chemo church" was born.

25

People flocked to him because he gave encouragement, hope, prayer, laughter, and optimism. Doctors would tell patients, "You need to go see Pastor Mike in room 305." Many people gave their hearts and lives to Jesus because Mike Fechner was ready in season and out of season.

Next Step

Believers are called to share the gospel with anyone, anywhere, and at any time. We are to "be ready" to share with everyone because we do not know whom God will chose for us. But in order to "be ready," we need to put ourselves in places to have those opportunities and pray for the opportunity to be used by God for His purpose.

Take your "Name List" and pray right now that God would use you today or this week to have a gospel conversation with them. Tell a close friend what you are doing and ask them to keep you accountable to your plans. You will be amazed how your motivation to reach the lost will increase when you know that you will soon tell your friend the results of your encounter.

After having prayed, make plans to put yourself in front of the people on your name list. Do not be passive. You must actively insert yourself into their lives. But get ready! God is about to use you in some incredible ways!

What can you do specifically in the next seven days to give yourself a chance to be used by God in the lives of the people in your Name List?

_____

_____

_____

Chapter Three
Evangelism Your Way

I work in the office next to Reverend Sal Barone. This man lives and breathes evangelism. Whenever and wherever he meets someone, he will quickly transition the conversation to spiritual matters. But he is rarely one to leave an encounter without asking, "Are you ready to give your heart to Jesus?" Quite often the response he gets is "Yes."

After leading a person to the Lord, Sal would often give me their name and contact information for follow up. In the first year of this pattern, I would have a strange mix of emotions. On the one hand I was elated that I have a new brother or sister in Christ that I could help grow in their new faith. But I was also strangely discouraged. Why does evangelism come so easily for Sal? Why is he leading so many people to the Lord and I am struggling just to have a full "Name List?" What does he think about me and my comparable lack of evangelistic fruit?

Eventually I came to realize two important truths. First, my thought process was selfish. Christians are not meant to compare results and outcomes. Paul addressed this in First Corinthians chapter three. Some members of the church were devoted to Apollos and others were devoted to Paul. They were driven to strife as they compared the two brothers and their ministry "trophies." Paul rebuked them, saying,

What then is Apollos? What is Paul? Servants through whom you believed, as the Lord assigned to each. I planted, Apollos watered, but God gave the growth. So neither he who plants nor he who waters is anything, but only God who gives the growth. (1 Corinthians 3:5-7)

Paul affirms the role of each Christian in the conversion and spiritual development of new believers. Each are important in their varying roles.

Secondly, I realized that God gives certain believers a particular disposition toward evangelism. God gave Sal the spiritual gift of sharing the gospel of Jesus Christ. Not only is Sal very good at sharing, he also craves the opportunity to tell people about Jesus. Should I despair at this glorious gift that God has given Sal? By no means! But should I also sit idly by and let him do all the work? Again, by no means! Sal and I are *both* team members united with a common desire to fulfill the Great Commission. We are both called to seek the lost so that they may be saved. I celebrate that God has given Sal a particular gifting in evangelism and seek to partner with him on our road to glory.

Do you know of anyone that is particularly effective at sharing the gospel? What can you learn from them?

_____

_____

_____

God Made You Unique

God designed each of His children to be useful and effective in His mission to seek and save the lost. Allow me to make this more personal. God created you – in all of your glorious uniqueness – to be a useful and effective messenger of the gospel. Evangelism is not just for the evangelists. It is not just for Sal and all of his bold and extroverted friends. God made you unique and wants to use your unique characteristics to make known His plan of salvation.

> God created you – in all of your glorious uniqueness – to be a useful and effective messenger of the Gospel.

Sometimes God will use people who are obviously gifted in appearance and speech. King David was described as "a man of valor, a man of war, prudent in speech, and a man of good presence" (1 Samuel 16:18). Daniel was "skillful in all wisdom, endowed with knowledge" (Daniel 1:4). But God also used people without extraordinary intellect or speaking skills. Moses described himself as "not eloquent" and "slow of speech and of tongue" (Exodus 4:10). The Samaritan woman at the well was an unlikely person chosen by God to go into her hometown and tell everyone about Jesus.

God made you unique and wants to use your unique attributes to tell the world about His Son Jesus. The Apostle Paul put it this way:

For we are his workmanship, created in Christ Jesus for good works, which God prepared beforehand, that we should walk in them. (Ephesians 2:10)

The Greek word for "workmanship" is *poema*. It is the same Greek word where we get the English word poem. You and I are the ultimate expressions of His creativity. But keep in mind that He designed us with a purpose. We are created and designed to be ambassadors of His Kingdom in a way that nobody else can. If you are an introvert, God designed you that way to do His work through that personality. Similarly, if you are an extrovert, God wants you to use your unique ability of socializing with others for His Kingdom purposes.

Consider the way God used these people to fulfill His "good works, which God prepared beforehand."[viii]

Peter's "Bull in a China Shop" Approach – Peter did not hesitate to tell you exactly what he thought. His personality made him famous as he declared boldly to Jesus, "You are the Christ, the Son of the living God" (Matthew 16:15). He was willing to jump out of the boat when he saw Jesus walking on water. God used Peter mightily on Pentecost to take a stand in the very city that Jesus was crucified. Three thousand people trusted Christ and became believers that day.

Paul's "Shakespeare" Approach – Paul was both eloquent and an intellectual. His writings in the New Testament are some of the most difficult literature that you will come across. Peter says of his letters, "There are some things in them that are hard to understand" (2 Peter

3:16). But God used Paul's eloquence and intellect to argue point-counterpoint with Roman officials, prosecutors, and philosophers.

The Blind Man's "Testimony" Approach – The blind man healed by Jesus in John 9 was not an intellect. He was not accustomed to commanding the attention of large crowds. But he had a story to tell. When pressed by Pharisees to explain the situation, he said, "One thing I do know, that though I was blind, now I see" (John 9:25). Who could deny such a claim?

Matthew's "Inner Circle" Approach – Matthew was a surprising convert to Christianity because he was a tax collector by trade. These men were notoriously crooked and held close fellowship with one another because friends were scarce outside of their profession. After accepting Jesus' call to become one of His followers, Matthew strategically pursued his friends for Christ. The Scriptures say Matthew threw "a great feast in his house" (Luke 5:29) and invited all of his tax collector friends to hear Jesus in person.

The Samaritan Woman's "Y'all Come See" Approach – The Samaritan woman was surprised by Jesus at a well. In that unconventional encounter, she came to realize that Jesus was the Messiah. Her life would never be the same. She ran back to her hometown and said, "Come, see a man who told me all that I ever did. Can this be the Christ?" (John 4:29). The Scripture records that many did come and they "believed in him because of the woman's testimony" (John 4:39).

Dorcas's "Lifestyle" Approach – Dorcas was well known for her service and kind deeds. The Bible says she was "full of good works and acts of charity" (Acts 9:36). Her kindness was used by God to bring attention to her life and point people to Jesus.

Which of these approaches do you most identify with? Why?

_____

_____

_____

Find Your Approach

The Scripture is abundantly clear that Christians are to actively share their faith. Evangelism is not an option. It is mandated from Jesus Christ Himself. Believers are ambassadors of His Kingdom to a lost and dying world. Make no mistake about it. The church is losing its grip on influencing the culture because believers do not feel the weight of the directive to share their faith.

I believe one reason so many believers are not sharing their faith is because they do not recognize the many forms it takes. Evangelism is not strictly engaging a stranger with a pre-cooked outline. It comes in a variety of methods and approaches. As we just learned, Peter shared his faith with thousands at one time just like Dorcas shared her faith to many through her good works. Paul engaged the intellects just like Matthew gathered his friends. They are all legitimate forms of evangelism as long as they point a person to the gospel.

> Your personality, experiences, and passions all form a blueprint for you to find your evangelism approach.

God made you unique. Your personality, experiences, and passions all form a blueprint for you to find your evangelism approach. Consider the following approaches and decide which from the list best match your personality profile.

The Bull in a China Shop – This form of evangelism is for the believer that prefers to just look a person in the eye and ask them where they stand with Jesus. It is confrontational and often bold. But it is done with a heart of compassion and love. This is Dr. Don Wilton's favorite form of evangelism. He enjoys quickly getting to the question, "Do you want to give you heart to Jesus today?" He does not feel the need to necessarily get to know the person or win their permission. He wants to know where they stand for eternity and, if needed, lead them to eternal life with Jesus.

If this approach matches your personality, there is a good chance you have the gift of evangelism. God uses these "evangelists" to reach many people. If you think this is you, ask the Holy Spirit to guide you to know how, when, and where to direct your gifting. Also ask for wisdom to share your faith with a right mix of grace and truth.

The Storyteller – God has masterfully told His story of redemption through sixty-six books and many authors. He has woven a masterpiece beginning with creation, continuing through the fall of man, climaxing with the death, burial, and resurrection of Jesus, and culminating with the apocalyptic Second Coming.

God also made millions of storytellers to beautifully narrate how the gospel changes everything. This form of evangelism is for the believer who enjoys telling others his or her story of redemption. The storyteller uses his or her testimony to point people to Christ. Everyone should be ready, willing, and able to share their story of coming to Christ, but the storyteller seeks out opportunities to give their testimony.

The Lawyer – Some believers are particularly adept at making the case for Christ. This method is for the believer that can effectively win an argument. The Apostle Paul could go toe-to-toe with the greatest intellects of his day. He could also change his approach and speak persuasively to a different audience. But he was always using his mind to figure out how to give a convincing argument to win people to the Lord.

This method is not just for lawyers. It is a method for those who enjoy persuading people of their opinion. If you particularly relish proving your sports team is better, you may be a "lawyer." If you engage others in discussions about politics and social changes, you may be just the right person to persuade others to the Lord. But remember that very few people are "argued" into the Kingdom. This method must always be seasoned with grace and compassion.

The Networker – Some people have lots of friends and acquaintances. You will find them on Facebook because they have over one thousand "friends" and will be happy to update you on their day's progress. The Networker is friendly, often extroverted, likeable, and social.

A lady at the church I attend is seen bringing people with her to church all the time. She is not a theological giant. She can be a little rough around the edges. But she is a Networker and she uses her personality profile to bring others to faith in Jesus.

The Do-Gooder – Jesus said, "let your light shine before others, so that they may see your good works and give glory to your Father who is in heaven" (Matthew 5:16). God wants all believers to do good works because they can point people to Him. But the Do-Gooder is intentional and strategic. He or she will do a benevolent gesture with the aim to lead the non-believer down a path toward the gospel.

It has been said that the things you do speak louder than the things you say. The Do-Gooder agrees. Peter told a group of scattered and persecuted Christians, "Keep your conduct among the Gentiles honorable, so that when they speak against you as evildoers, they may see your good deeds and glorify God on the day of visitation" 1 Peter 2:12). This may be your method if you are hesitant to start a conversation that contains theology but you are more than happy to go the extra mile (Matthew 5:41) in order that people will see Christ in you. But keep in mind that simply doing good deeds is not sharing your faith. But the good deeds lead to a gospel conversation.

The Introvert – In many ways I hope this book will be helpful for the introvert. I can easily relate to this group. The idea of talking with someone about a subject that may cause an unpredictable response can be frightful. I would much rather have a gospel conversation over email than over the phone. I am thought oriented and do best when I have time to respond to challenging questions or rebuttals. Never the less, the introvert has a place in the world of evangelism.

Introverts have some unique advantages in evangelism. Often introverts are in tune with feelings and are sensitive in their approach. Introverts are the best people to reach other introverts. Research says introverts make up over half of the population. A "bull in a china shop" will often scare off those that do not appreciate confrontation. But an introvert can reach other quiet people who think deeply.

Again, God made you unique. Your personality, experiences, and passions all form a blueprint for you to find your evangelism approach. Although the evangelistic approaches listed above are not exhaustive, they give an idea of how you might use your unique blend of characteristics and experiences to participate in the Great Commission. Which of the above approaches best match your personality profile?

_____

_____

_____

Play the Game

I used to be confused why the manager of a baseball team is dressed in the team uniform during the games. He does not get to make plays on the field or takes swings at the pitches. Why would he be in a baseball uniform? But then I coached a little league baseball team. The coach is absolutely very much a part of the game. He is making decisions that are crucial for the outcome of the game. He is motivating his players. He is working with the umpires to keep the game fair. He is the puppet master behind the scenes that nobody notices. The manager absolutely plays the game.

Conversely, a baseball player can be in uniform, on the field, and in the line up, but not playing the game. As the coach of a little league team, I am constantly trying to keep my players engaged with the game. They are children and often distracted by parents, friends, and even

34

butterflies. When the ball is hit their way, they snap back to reality, but it is often too late. The ball quickly rolls right by them.

All Christians have been drafted onto God's team, given the uniform, and put on the field. But being on the field does not mean that you are playing the game. God has given Christians the game plan. But we cannot merely look the part. We cannot just go through the motions of Sunday morning worship, small groups, and Bible studies without taking part in evangelism.

Furthermore, evangelism is not simply living a moral life and doing good deeds for the less fortunate. Those are both very important and central to being obedient to Christ. But evangelism requires words. The Bible says, "How are they to believe in him of whom they have never heard? And how are they to hear without someone preaching?" (Romans 10:14). In order for a person to believe, someone must be sent to that person to share the words of the gospel.

A famous quote often attributed to St. Francis of Assisi is "Preach the gospel, and if necessary, use words." With all due respect to Francis, using words is *always* necessary to preach the gospel. Of course his point is that our lifestyle should be evidence of a life changed by the gospel. But too often the quote has been misapplied to mean that verbalizing the plan of salvation is not necessary. On the contrary, Christians must use their godly lifestyle as a bridge to share their faith.

When was the last time you actually shared God's plan of salvation with another person? Let this question sink in and be honest. You are not too old or too young to share your faith with another person. You may be busy with many good activities. But are you playing the game? Or are you in uniform, on the field, and distracted by the butterflies?

Next Step

First, you need to embrace your evangelism approach. God has made you unique. You are His workmanship, His masterpiece, and His poem. He is very pleased with how He made you. Now live within the

35

framework you were given. Use your personality, experiences, and interests to lead people to Christ. Do not try to be someone you are not.

No one can reach certain people as well as you can. This is your responsibility and therefore becomes a stewardship issue. God has put certain people in your path for *you* to reach. You are perfectly designed to reach them. Now go out and play the game!

Second, you need someone in your life to help keep you focused. I list this step again because it is so important. Tell a close friend what you are doing and ask them to keep you accountable to your plans. You will be amazed how your motivation to reach the lost will increase when you know that you will soon tell your friend the results of your encounter. Additionally, your close friend will also feel compelled to participate with you!

At this point, you ought to do the following steps:

1. Create a "Name List." This is a short list of names of people that you suspect do not know Jesus as their Lord and Savior.

2. Pray daily that God would use you today or this week to have a gospel conversation with them.

3. Embrace your evangelistic approach. Think through how God made you. Now how can you best reach people given your unique characteristics and experiences?

4. Tell a close friend your intentions to have gospel conversations with your name list. Plan on telling your friend the results of your efforts on a weekly basis.

Ready, set, GO!!

Chapter Four
The Power of Proximity

Entrepreneur Ruben Chavez is credited with saying, "The person you will be in five years depends largely on the information you feed your mind today. Be picky about the books you read, the people you spend time with, and the conversations you engage in."[ix] There is a good bit of truth to what he says. We are largely influenced by the people with whom we spend time, the books we read, and the media we digest. For instance, your worldview is largely impacted if you watch MSNBC or Fox News multiple hours every day. Additionally, you are significantly influenced by the amount of time you give to reading your Bible. Who are you giving permission to speak into your life on a regular basis?

> Your compassion for the lost is in direct proportion to the amount of time you spend with lost people.

Your compassion for the lost is in direct proportion to the amount of time you spend with lost people. Those who have isolated themselves from meaningful time with unbelievers typically do not have a burning desire to reach the lost for Christ. Conversely, Christians who spend quality time with unbelievers often will have a burden to reach them for Christ. Why? The Holy Spirit softens the heart of the believer to have compassion for the lost. If believers are never around lost people, their hearts are not regularly softened to reach the lost.

There is a power inherent with proximity. The things we choose to have proximity to our minds and hearts will impact us. For instance, if you work in close proximity with a coworker, you will probably care if they have a death in the family. But if you have not worked with that same coworker for ten years, you probably will not be impacted much. This is the same person. The only difference is proximity. We care about the people who occupy our time. If you care about reaching the lost, you will spend time with them.

Salt and Light

Jesus understood the power of proximity. He used a famous metaphor to emphasize the importance of being near the lost. He said:

[13] "You are the salt of the earth, but if salt has lost its taste, how shall its saltiness be restored? It is no longer good for anything except to be thrown out and trampled under people's feet.
[14] "You are the light of the world. A city set on a hill cannot be hidden.[15] Nor do people light a lamp and put it under a basket, but on a stand, and it gives light to all in the house. [16] In the same way, let your light shine before others, so that they may see your good works and give glory to your Father who is in heaven." (Matthew 5:13-16)

Christian, you are the salt of the earth. Do you know what that means? Most of us readily grasp the concept of being the light of the world. Many can easily recite the words to "This Little Light of Mine." But what does it mean to be the salt of the earth?

In the ancient world salt was one of the most common substances. Roman soldiers were paid with salt and would riot if they did not get their ration. Our English word "salary" comes from the Latin *salarium* literally meaning "salt-money."[x]

Salt did not have value simply because it added flavor to food. Rather salt was valuable because it kept meat from decaying. The ancients would rub down meat and fish to preserve it. Even today people who live "off the grid" and do not have a refrigerator will use salt to dry or cure meat. One camping lifestyle magazine says, "Dried meat will last indefinitely" if done correctly.[xi] You can imagine how valuable salt would be prior to the invention of refrigerators.

But Jesus was not necessarily talking about the monetary value of salt. He was referencing its ability to impede the decaying process. The world around us is rotting and decaying. Jesus calls upon Christians to be pervasive in the world and keep it from completely imploding! Consider some of the ways Jesus modeled being salt.

Adoption

In the first century, children did not have much value. Many were often viewed as a drain. But Jesus, though having no children of his own, loved children. He rebuked the disciples for blocking the children from coming to him. Instead Jesus "took them in his arms and blessed them, laying his hands on them" (Mark 10:16). The early church took Jesus' example and became salt. They began adopting children that were rejected from their homes and cast aside. This has continued throughout the last two thousand years. Today Christian men and women largely lead the movement of adopting and fostering children.

Women's Rights

Jesus was absolutely revolutionary with His view of women. In the first century, women were essentially the property of their husbands. They could be mistreated and abused with no legal recourse. But Jesus included women in His ministry and even His closest circle of friends. He elevated the status of women and gave them the dignity and respect they deserve. Historically wherever Christianity spread, the respect and worth of women followed. Even today we see the cultures with the worst record for women's right (ie. Yemen, Pakistan, Chad, and Syria) also lack a significant Christian influence.

Health Care and Relief Organizations

Anyone who reads the gospels will conclude that Jesus loved people with ailments. He was more than happy to go out of His way or be interrupted in order to minister to the sick. The Church has followed that example. For instance, at the Council of Nicea in 325AD, churches were implored to open a corresponding hospital everywhere a church was started. During the great plague, Christians signed up to care for the sick at great risk because they knew that if they got sick and died they would go be with Jesus. Even today many hospitals are Baptist, Presbyterian, or Catholic in origin. With a trained volunteer force exceeding eighty thousand people, the Southern Baptist Disaster Relief fuels the third largest disaster relief agency in the United States.

Each of these examples is of Christians being salt to a dying and morally decadent world. John Stott points out, "When society does go bad, we Christians tend to throw up our hands in pious horror and reproach the non-Christian world; but should we not rather reproach ourselves? One can hardly blame unsalted meat for going bad. It cannot do anything else. The real question to ask is: where is the salt?"[xii]

The key to being salt is proximity. You cannot be salt from a distance. You have to be involved and engrossed in the lives of people. Where is the salt?

Draw Near Unto Them

If we are going to reach our world for Christ, the most effective way is through friendships. Quick question: Are you more influenced by a person you just met sitting next to you on an airplane or by a friend you have gotten to know over time? You are probably far more inclined to seriously consider the words of a friend more than someone you just met. In the same way, you are going to have much greater success sharing about your spiritual experience with a friend than you are with a stranger.

Our culture is becoming increasingly divided. Not only are Christians retreating to their places of comfort, unbelievers are also not hanging out with Bible-believing Christians. This "us-and-them" mentality is seriously damaging evangelistic efforts. Some churches have tried to mend the gap by offering attractive worship services that resemble a pop concert. While I applaud efforts to remove barriers to the gospel, making the worship service a primary means of outreach is not a biblical recipe for reaching the lost. I cannot find any biblical author exhorting the church elders to make the worship service more attractive to unbelievers. The normal mode of transferring the faith is from one person to the next.

If we are going to reach our world for Christ, the most effective way is through friendships.

The most natural and effective way to reach the lost is through friendships. Christians must overcome their tendency to seek refuge from the world and instead penetrate the darkness with gospel light. In short, we need to get close to them and show them that we genuinely care.

The act of getting close to a nonbeliever is more like a discipline. It requires a game plan, resolve, and possibly also goal setting. It has similarities to being on a diet. Any serious dieter knows he or she must be committed, plan strategically, and set goals. The same is true for befriending the lost. You must set out with a plan, be committed to the plan, and be willing to evaluate your success.

This chapter will help you with your game plan. All effective plans have a good place to start. Consider this your starting point. Below you will find several simple but effective ways to begin this journey. The end goal is for you to begin a new friendship with a nonbeliever for the primary purpose to lead them to Christ, because you genuinely care for that person.

Practice One: Bless

In my home state of Texas I grew up hearing the phrase, "Bless his heart." Apparently that euphemism contained too many words. In South Carolina the term is shortened to just "Bless." Generally speaking it is used to express a desire to confer blessing or prosperity upon someone who is often in a difficult situation. When my son in his first grade body was playing basketball against a fourth grade boy, the common refrain from bleacher parents was "Bless."

Similarly Christians will make a tremendous impact if they are willing to genuinely bless someone – to bring happiness to their life usually by way of relieving them of a burden. This includes any generous act that will lift their spirit or alleviate their distress.

Recently a friend of mine used the discipline of "blessing" to reach a new neighbor. He lives out in the country and periodically takes his fallen tree branches to be mulched. As he was pulling out of his driveway he noticed his neighbor was doing yard work. Up to this point my friend had not had any lengthy conversations with the neighbor. He only knew that he was from the north and did not attend a church regularly. My friend pulled up to his neighbor and offered to take his brush pile. The neighbor was apparently quite surprised by the generous offer since he was not accustomed to such kind offers. My friend "doubled-down" on the occasion and said that when he got back he was going to bring over a freshly baked apple pie his wife had just made. Soon the two couples were engaged in a lovely conversation and a friendship was born. This friendship opened opportunities to have gospel conversations with the husband.

The act of blessing comes in as many forms as the imagination can conceive. But you must imagine the many ways you can bless. Your life of salty holiness may be your biggest contribution to this world. You may not be a preacher, teacher, or influential leader. But remember that Jesus spent the first thirty years of His life content to live a life of holiness. Perhaps God is calling you to live a public life of radical obedience to Him for the salvation of many.

If this practice of blessing others resonates with your heart, I encourage you to set yourself a goal. As a recommendation, set out each week to bless three people – at least two of whom are not members of your church. Log your results on a notepad and then watch how God uses your unusual kindness to draw people unto Him.

Practice two: Breaking Bread

I do not know the reason, but Americans seem to have become increasingly pragmatic about their meals. We have made it about the function of filling our stomachs. Most restaurants offer the ability for patrons to quickly get food to go. They also seem to be offering fewer tables with seating with more than four chairs. In many houses, the dining room has become the museum for china and glassware. Modern houses are not even being built with a distinct dining room even though the size of the average home built today is considerably larger than those built in earlier decades.[xiii]

42

But in many other cultures, meals are an occasion to break bread with family, neighbors, friends, and strangers. Whenever I hear stories of Americans that go on short-term international mission trips, they all seem to be startled at the importance their hosts place on eating meals together. Throughout much of history, gathering at the dinner table has been an occasion to share both food and time together.

Bill Hybels tells the story of Mark – a church member eager to bring someone to his church's weeklong evangelistic outreach. Mark bought four tickets. Two were for he and his wife and the other two were for his guests. Mark had the young couple next door on his heart. They were not married, had shown no inclination towards spiritual matters, and he only knew them by their first names. Mark saw them in their yard and took the occasion to invite them. The young couple responded, "Um...thanks anyway, but I don't think we will go this time. But, well, if you'd ever like to get together in the backyard for a barbecue, let us know."

Hybels suggests an important principle: you've got to barbecue first![xiv] The culture we live in is full of people and businesses with an agenda. In order to break through the initial distrust, you have to pay the relational rent. That rent is particularly payable in the form of a meal together. In order to get most people to accept your invitation to the church service or a church event, you need to establish a relationship on natural, nonthreatening grounds. Then, later in the context of a mutual friendship, you can open up about spiritual matters and have great success.

Now it is time to put this great theory into practice. If you believe in the power of breaking bread, set a goal to eat with at least one person every week that you think may be far from God. Again, for many people, they need to share pulled pork with you before they share the pew with you. So fire up the grill, dust off your cookbook, and start praying about who you can invite to your dinner table.

Practice three: Reposition Yourself

God cannot bless what you are not doing. Many Christians have positioned their lives to have minimal contact with the spiritually lost people in this world. In order for God to bless your evangelistic efforts, you must first reposition yourself to be around unbelievers.

> God cannot bless what you are not doing.

Recently I was invited to join the board of a little league baseball association. My initial thought was, "Why would I willingly sign up for something that will add to my busy schedule, require me to be a peacemaker for irrational parents, and inevitably gain me some enemies because it is easy to hate the ones making the decisions?" Additionally, as I met with some of the other board members, the language thrown around caused me to cringe. But rather than view this invitation as a burden, I saw it as an opportunity given to me from God.

I accepted the board position for the primary reason of repositioning myself to have more influence in the lives of the lost. Of course I will gladly make every effort to continue the existing high level of quality leadership. I will work towards improving the league in any way I can. But my hard work and commitment is the groundwork for establishing trust, favor, and a good reputation in the community. Prayerfully this will be the foundation for opportunities God will send me to have spiritual conversations.

The point here is that you need to be willing to be inconvenienced for the sake of the gospel. You need to join that club or take that leadership role. You need to invite those lost friends to your dominoes night. You need to join the PTA or the booster club. You need to expand the list of people you include for your golf foursome. You need to volunteer at places like the local pregnancy care center, the homeless shelter, the soup kitchen, and medical clinics. The good you do at each of these places is an expression of God's love toward people whom God loves. But God's love cannot be fully expressed without sharing with them His greatest expression of love; namely, "God shows his love for us in that while we were still sinners, Christ died for us" (Romans 5:8).

Perhaps in the reading of this chapter God has put on your heart something you know you need to do. Make a goal to take steps towards accomplishing that task. Tell your spouse or a friend your plans and ask them to hold you accountable to taking steps in that direction. If nothing has come to mind, begin praying regularly for God to open opportunities to reposition your life for the sake of the gospel.

Practice Four: Listen

Coaching a baseball team of five– and six–year–olds can feel like an exercise in futility. On one occasion I told the center fielder that the ball was probably going to be hit to him and he needed to be ready to throw it in to second base. Sure enough the ball was hit right to him. I said in a firm voice, "Throw the ball." Then I saw him running with the ball. I said in a louder – still firm – voice, "Throw the ball!" At this point he was full speed running to second base. I hollered as loud as my voice would allow literally feet from his ear, "TIIROW THE BALL!". My efforts were in vain. The boy ran from the outfield to second base with a look of pure satisfaction.

I wonder how often the Holy Spirit is in our ear pleading for us to stop, move, run, etc. How many more times would we have opportunities for gospel conversations if we just practiced the art of listening to God? Remember, my friend would not have stopped to talk to his neighbor if he was not in tune with the Spirit who prompted Him to lend a hand.

Listening to the Spirit can be like trying to hear a song in a busy restaurant. You know a song is being played over the speakers. Parts of the song sound familiar. But you have to strain to have a chance to hear the song enough to know the singer and song title. The same thing can happen with the Holy Spirit. Too many people and other things can interfere. We need a way to tune out the interference and listen to God's voice. We simply need to learn how to listen.

In Isaiah 6, the prophet is in tune with God. Isaiah "heard the voice of the Lord saying, 'Whom shall I send, and who will go for us?' Then [Isaiah] said, 'Here I am! Send me.'" He was listening with the heart and was able to respond in obedience. The practice of listening requires being alert, observant, and perceptive to what is going on within us and around us. Listening is not a passive action but a conscious, willed action to focus attention.

David Mathis, author and the Executive Director of DesiringGod.org, says good listening requires patience. "Perhaps we think we know where the speaker is going, and so already begin formulating our response. Or we were in the middle of something when someone started talking to us, or have another commitment approaching, and we wish they were done already." This is certainly true for those of us prone to tasks or excuses. "When we are people quick to speak, it takes Spirit-powered patience to not only be quick to hear, but to keep on hearing."[xv]

If you want to reach the lost, you need to get busy listening to God. As a point of action, consider ways you might need to silence unnecessary distractions. Is your phone buzzing you with traffic reports or sports scores? Is that music in your car helping you hear from God? Is your daily schedule so packed that you are constantly running from one place to the next? Tune out the distractions and tune into God.

Next Step

The best way to reach the lost is to get near them. With the culture increasingly at odds with biblical Christianity, Christians are trending towards isolationism. We retreat and sometimes mock them. This creates a dangerous mindset. Jesus did the opposite. He drew near unto them and had compassion upon them.

I suggested four practices to draw near to them along with some reasonable goals:

1. **Bless them.** Set out each week to bless three people – at least two of whom are not members of your church. Log your results on a notepad and then watch how God uses your unusual kindness to draw people unto Him.

2. **Break bread with them.** Set a goal to eat with at least one person every week that you think may be far from God. Breakfast, lunch, dinner, coffee, and desert all work well.

3. **Reposition yourself.** Begin praying regularly for God to open opportunities to reposition your life for the sake of the gospel. What can you do to put yourself in the stream of lost people more often?

4. **Listen.** Consider ways you might need to silence unnecessary distractions. Tune out the distractions and tune into God.

Chapter Five
You are Not Alone

The entire evangelism process is a supernatural journey. Last year my daughter was in the third grade. She had a particularly charismatic boy in her class that we all sensed was special. So our family made intentional attempts to get to know him and his family. His teacher – a wonderful Christian lady – also joined in praying for him.

Recently my family went to a restaurant and him in the parking lot. We sparked up conversation and discovered that his mom worked next door. So we invited the boy to join us for lunch. Keep in mind, I was tired from a hectic morning. But part of evangelism is making yourself available whenever God brings opportunities along. We all immediately felt compelled to invite him to the upcoming church summer camp. Camp was expensive for a last-minute invitation and the church was out of scholarships. But I still pleaded with the leaders to find a way. Lo and behold, a scholarship opened up and he was able to attend.

At this point, we had seen God burden our hearts for the young man. His teacher was doing her part praying for him and showing him Jesus. My wife had particularly gone out of her way to establish trust with his mom. I got over my selfishness and invited him to join us for lunch and we pulled the trigger by inviting him. He came to camp with an open heart. He was captivated by the entire experience. On the third day of camp, he sought out his camp counselor and asked how he could surrender his life to Jesus!

Did you see how active God was in the entire process? You would probably be amazed to see how many variables are supernaturally working together behind the scenes. The important principle to remember is that you are not alone. You are not on a solo mission. Your efforts toward pointing a person to the gospel initiates an entire operation headed by the Trinity – God the Father, God the Son, and God the Holy Spirit! Would you not be more courageous knowing that the fullness of God is working with you every step of the way? Let's discover how this evangelistic operation works.

Jesus is With You Always

Jesus gave us the marching orders. He said, "Go therefore and make disciples of all nations" (Matthew 28:19a). This commissioning must have been mind-boggling to Jesus' disciples. They had just seen the Jews and the Roman authorities put the most innocent man that had ever lived on the cross to be executed. The one person who had never done an evil deed in his life had just been sent to where the most evil people go to publicly die. Not only are the disciples called to continue His message, but also bring in others to follow Jesus.

The disciples knew they were going to have a very hard time continuing Jesus' message without Him healing the sick, speaking the truth, and loving everyone. But Jesus essentially said, "We will not convert the world just by staying here and being good. Most people will not come running to us. You need to go out, bring them in, and teach them what it means to follow Me. That is your central and most critical task as the Church." The disciples must have been shaking in their sandals.

But Jesus' final words of the Great Commission were and are amazing. He said as you do it, as you go, as you work your way through history, through all the things you do, remember this: "I am with you always, to the end of the age" (Matthew 28:20b). The Son of God, the Lion of Judah, the King of Kings, our Hope, our Redeemer, the Supreme Creator over all is with you always!

St. Patrick – yes, the same one who gets celebrated every April – is known for bringing the gospel to Ireland. To say that he single-handedly turned Ireland from a pagan to a Christian country is an exaggeration, but it is not far from the truth. During his extensive missionary journeys, Patrick wrote poems and hymns. He understood that Christ was with him always. He wrote in his poem *Lorica*:

Christ with me, Christ before me, Christ behind me,
Christ in me, Christ beneath me, Christ above me,
Christ on my right, Christ on my left,

Christ when I lie down,
Christ when I sit down,
Christ when I arise,
Christ in the heart of every man who thinks of me,
Christ in the mouth of every one who speaks of me,
Christ in the eye of every one who sees me,
Christ in every ear that hears me.   St. Patrick (ca. 377)

I really cannot think of a more beautiful way of putting it. When you reach that point of opportunity to have a gospel conversation, you can be assured that Jesus has gone before you, will go after you, is in your words, your eyes, your mind, and with you in every way. As we go forth with our mission on earth, rest assured Jesus is "with you always, to the end of the age."

The Spirit Speaks to their Heart

My first job in high school was being a telemarketer (don't hate me!). I was a sixteen year old, having just finished my sophomore year of high school, and I was tasked to make cold calls selling accidental death insurance! I had to call people who had never expressed an interest in accidental death insurance and try to convince them that they would regret passing up my silly offer. I was envious of the coworkers that were calling people that had expressed interest in their product. Evangelism is never a "cold call." While you are establishing relationships with your lost friends, neighbors, and coworkers, the Holy Spirit is actively working in their lives and preparing them for your gospel conversation. By the time you come along, the Spirit has been long at work.

Before the Lord led Peter to speak with Cornelius, the Holy Spirit was already at work preparing the way. If you look at Acts 10:1-15, you can see that God was orchestrating every detail on both sides to bring Peter and Cornelius together. Yet Peter had no clue why he was going to Caesarea and Cornelius did not know what Peter was going to say. The point is that the Holy Spirit was busy at work in the lives of both Peter –

50

a Christian – and Cornelius – a nonbeliever – to bring them both to a time and place where the gospel would be proclaimed.

The Holy Spirit prepares the way by bringing a conviction of sin. Jesus said the Holy Spirit has come to "convict the world concerning sin and righteousness and judgment" (John 16:8). The Holy Spirit in essence convicts sinners of what is wrong, what is right, and what happens to those who do wrong and do right! Whenever you begin praying about engaging a lost person with the gospel, you can be assured that the Holy Spirit is already actively at work softening their heart and bringing a restlessness about their standing with God. It may not be evident, but you can believe it is happening deep within their soul.

While the Holy Spirit is working in the life of your lost friend or neighbor, simultaneously the Spirit is also empowering you. Before Jesus ascended into Heaven, He told His disciples in Acts 1:8, "But you will receive power when the Holy Spirit has come upon you, and you will be my witnesses in Jerusalem and in all Judea and Samaria, and to the end of the earth." The word *power* refers to all the help or aid which the Holy Spirit grants such as the power of speaking the gospel with great effect, the power of having spiritual intuition, and receiving courage when you are feeling uncertain.

In short, the Holy Spirit is absolutely foundational to all evangelistic efforts. You are not alone. You always have the Spirit with you. The Scripture says that

- He empowers you to witness (Acts 1:8)
- He gives you wisdom (Luke 12:12)
- He gives you boldness (Acts 4:31)
- He helps you in your praying (Romans 8:26)
- He gives you the burning desire to see people saved (Acts 4:29-31)

How have you seen or felt the Holy Spirit move in your own life as it relates to evangelism?

_____

_____

_____

God Does the Saving

I have what I think will be excellent news for you. Your lost family member, friend, or neighbor is not going to heaven or hell because of you. Their eternal destiny is not contingent upon you saying the right words at the right time. You will not be held responsible for anyone's spiritual status before God. "Salvation belongs to the Lord" (Psalm 3:8).

Our great privilege is that God uses us to bring salvation to many. He could use fire from the sky, visions, dreams, or talking animals. But instead God uses us. That's His plan.

The second most popular verse in the Bible[xvi] is Jeremiah 29:11 which starts, "For I know the plans I have for you." We like the second half of the verse that says, "plans to prosper you and not to harm you, plans to give you hope and a future." It is true that God is for you and plans to give you all that you need for

> Our great privilege is that God uses us to bring salvation to many.

"life and godliness" (2 Peter 1:3). But His big plan for your life is for you to participate in the mission He gave you. You were made for a mission. God desires that all sinners be saved (1 Timothy 2:4; 2 Peter 3:9; Ezekiel 18:23; Matthew 23:37). Once a sinner is saved, he or she is then sent out into the world to share that great news to a lost and dying world.

If God is the author of salvation and sends out His children into the world to let them know about Jesus, surely God has equipped you to be good at telling His story. The central theme of this book is to help you see evangelism as not only our mission but also very feasible. Evangelism is feasible because God designed you to be able to do this.

So many of us get hung up with thoughts like, "I'm not good with words," "I don't know enough," and "I'm too old (or young)." Jeremiah objected to God appointing him as a prophet. He said, "Ah, Lord God! Behold, I do not know how to speak, for I am only a youth." But God responded, "Do not say, 'I am only a youth'; for to all to whom I send you, you shall go, and whatever I command you, you shall speak" (Jeremiah 1:6-7). Jeremiah was not the most obvious choice to speak for God. But he was God's choice. He was called and commissioned by God for a task...just like you.

Again, if this is God's plan for you (and it is), then He has equipped you to do it. Do not worry about the results. Leave those to God. He is the one who brings salvation. But God is sending you out as His special agent to talk to others about Him and let them know your own story of redemption and reconciliation.

In what ways do you think God has specifically made you to be His ambassador?

_____

_____

_____

Scripture Cuts to the Core

Your Bible is no mere collection of books written by many authors over centuries. Scripture is more powerful than we will ever know. It has a mystical dimension about it. There are supernatural powers contained within the words that make it distinct from all other literature ever written. As it relates to evangelism, Scripture is your tool to break through a hardened heart and bring salvation.

The author of Hebrews says of the Bible, "For the word of God is living and active, sharper than any two-edged sword, piercing to the division of soul and of spirit, of joints and of marrow, and discerning the thoughts and intentions of the heart" (Hebrews 4:12). The words in our Bibles are living and active. They are not dead and lifeless. The truths contained within bring forth life and power. As a young and troubled seminary professor being pursued by God, Martin Luther declared, "The Bible is alive, it speaks to me; it has feet, it runs after me; it has hands, it lays hold on me." What other book could do that?

The author painted a picture of the power within the pages of the Bible. He says the Word of God is sharper than a two-edged sword. Whereas a sword is often associated with battle, the description here is meant to draw out the imagery of a piercingly sharp object that is meant to easily cut through a tough substance.

The author further paints the picture of the Word of God by equating it to cutting through joints to get to the marrow. Joints are the thick, hard, outer part of the bone. Marrow is the soft, tender, living, inner part of the bone. The Word of God cuts through the hard, outer layer and penetrates to the core, piercing us with exacting precision.

The author gets more specific when he says the Word of God pierces "even to the division of soul and spirit." Although good scholars disagree about the exact meaning, the point seems to be that God's Word cuts through our bodily selves – our flesh – to our spiritual selves – our soul and spirit. We can deceive the world by dressing up our bodily selves. No one has to know what is going on inside and many of us can effectively hide our inner selves. But God's Word has the ability to break through our most potent defenses and cut to our core.

As it relates to evangelism, many of us have shied away from using the Bible because it is often mocked among seculars. We can also become hesitant to use it because of lack of familiarity or the possibility of being asked Bible-related tough questions. But keep a few important truths in mind. First, remember the power inherent within the Bible. It cuts to the very core of a person. It is a sharp, two-edged sword that will penetrate their heart. Second, in many cases, the Holy Spirit has already been preparing their hearts to interact with God's Word and lead them to the cross. Those who have ears to hear will hear and be affected. Finally, trust God in the process. The path to the cross is supernatural. It cannot be manufactured. Be obedient and watch God move!

Describe in your own words how scripture can cut to the core.

_____

_____

_____

We are Called to be Obedient

As we have seen, the fullness of God is working with you every step of the way. Evangelism is not a solo mission. But it absolutely requires our participation. We cannot allow the darkness to overcome the light in our community. If we continue to neglect our role, the world will see us as increasingly irrelevant.

Paul tells the Ephesian church (and us), "for at one time you were darkness, but now you are light in the Lord. Walk as children of light" (Ephesians 5:8). Our new identity calls for a new purpose. Are you still engaged with that purpose? Do you know what you are doing with your shining light?

The Scripture says that we are to "walk as children of the light." This demands that we both abstain from the elements of darkness and partake in a lifestyle of light. First, we are no longer free to do whatever the flesh chooses. We live according to a moral standard spelled out in God's Holy Word. That Word is authoritative – since it is from Almighty God – and dictates our moral choices. This includes what we say, what we eat and drink, how we conduct our business affairs, how we spend our money, and all the other choices we make in life. Frankly, God is not going to bless your evangelistic efforts if you are dabbling in the darkness.

Secondly, walking as children of the light means actively doing whatever pleases the Lord. The next verse helps us know what that means: "For the fruit of light is found in all that is good and right and true" (Ephesians 5:9). Goodness describes behavior that is others-oriented. A good person is always concerned for the well being of others, spiritually and in every way. Righteousness is living a life reflected of God's Holy character. It involves love, joy, peace, patience, etc. Finally living according to truth means declaring yourself aligned with God's truth. Christians stand opposed to Satan's lies that permeate our culture.

What does your shining light accomplish? Without light, there is nothing to contrast the darkness. In other words, light exposes darkness. Like most I have drifted into short seasons of straying from all that is good, right, and true. It has been the bright lights of friends and loved ones that remind me of Jesus and lead me back to the cross.

Similarly, if our lives are a dim light, our lost friends, neighbors, and coworkers will see no difference in their life and ours. They will have no remorse for unrighteousness, no concept of the need for forgiveness, and will probably conclude they are heading toward heaven just like you. In essence, a gospel conversation will make very little sense to them if they cannot see the light of Jesus in you.

Finally, living as a child in the light means you can help bring the darkness to light. Paul says a couple of verses later, "Awake, O sleeper, and arise from the dead, and Christ will shine on you" (Ephesians 5:14). When the light of the gospel comes in, it wakes up the spiritually dead and draws them to Jesus. As a child of the light, you help wake up the spiritually dead by being light.

What are some of the ways light affects darkness in the spiritual realm?

_____

_____

_____

Next Step

This book is designed to help you participate in God's mission to seek and save the lost. So as you are now over half the way through finishing this book, perhaps this is a good opportunity to keep you on track. By this time you ought to be:

1. **Maintaining and praying through your "name list."** This is a short list of names of people that you suspect do not know Jesus as their Lord and Savior. These names should come from your circle of relationships including your family, friends, neighbors, and co-workers. Pray daily for these people. If you meet in a small group or have some close friends, ask them to join you in praying for the people on the list.

2. **Making strategic plans to build trust or good will.** If your neighbor or coworker is on the list, do something to bring them joy. Be an active "light" in their life. If you have a friend or relative on the list, what can you do to build trust? Can you go out of your way and tell them you are praying for some difficulty in their life?

3. **Adding to your list.** Your life ought to be salty. But in order for salt to have its effect, you need to be around more lost people. What can you do to reposition your life in order to be around more lost people? Who can you add to your name list?

Chapter Six
Building Bridges

I am convinced that the guy who invented golf did not like people. Maybe he hated them. Golf is an absolutely maddening sport. Arnold Palmer said, "Golf is deceptively simple and endlessly complicated; it satisfies the soul and frustrates the intellect."[xvii]

Imagine a beautifully designed four hundred and fifty yard par four. You can blast a three hundred yard drive and then set yourself up with a nice layup just fifteen feet from the hole. Your putt positions you within three feet of the hole. Suddenly you are staring at three feet that will determine if you score a par or a bogey. Three simple feet count just as much as that three hundred yard beautiful drive and that picture perfect second shot onto the green. Three feet will determine if you have the satisfaction of scoring an enjoyable par or another irritating bogey. But the goal of the game is to get the golf ball into the hole. The first two shots were great, but the true satisfaction will not arrive until you hear the sound of the ball hitting the bottom of the cup.

You have laid all the groundwork. You have prayed for your lost friends, built a level of trust with them, blessed them, eaten with them, and made it known that you are a Christian. Congratulations! That is awesome and beautiful! Now it is time to sink the putt. Do not be satisfied with getting the ball close to the hole. That is not the goal. Your goal is to lead them to faith in Jesus Christ.

You need to build a gospel bridge. This is a transition from casual conversations to spiritual conversations. When a golfer is hitting a drive or a shot over a hundred yards from the green, he or she is not thinking about getting the ball in the hole. But as you get near the hole, you begin thinking about putting it in. The goal is in sight. But a gospel bridge needs a strategy. Your lost friend would be caught off guard if you went from talking college football to asking, "Do you know for sure that you are going to be with God in Heaven?" Alvin Reid, Senior Professor of Evangelism and Student Ministry at Southeastern Baptist Theological Seminary, suggests three simple approaches to building a bridge to a gospel conversation: explore, stimulate, and share.[xviii] This will provide a good framework to develop a strategy to start aiming for the goal!

Explore

Sometimes the best strategy is to begin exploring their spiritual background by asking tactical questions meant to drive the conversation to weightier subjects. For instance, if you have targeted a business partner, you can transition a lunch conversation to matters of real, daily life. You might say, "With work so crazy these days, how are you handling life at home?" This type of question is like a gentle knock at the door. You are asking to enter their life beyond the workplace. You are demonstrating that you care about more than just their ability to meet deadlines.

Generally speaking, we engage in three levels of talk: surface talk, personal talk, and spiritual talk (although these are broad categories and can overlap). A **surface level talk** often involves weather, sports, food, movies, news, etc. A **personal talk** will involve family, interests, ideas, and philosophies. It gives a glimpse of who they are as a person. A **spiritual talk** involves engaging a person from a spiritual standpoint. This is where you want to eventually arrive with the people on your name list. But it often takes moving from surface level to a personal level before you can engage them on a spiritual level. The movements from one level to the next are called gospel bridges.

A gospel bridge can come in the form of small seeds that you throw out. These are quick, subtle comments that are meant to gauge interest. For instance, if there is a new neighbor in town, a gospel bridge might sound like this: "We love this neighborhood. The grocery store is right around the corner. There is a great park with walking trails and our church is only three blocks from here." This is a natural conversation that you have included a little gospel seed to assess their reaction.

I occasionally use social media as a gospel bridge to specifically reach one person. A friend on my name list is a parent and had some strong opinions about parenting. But he did not attend church with his family and I suspected he was not a believer. He did, however, peruse Facebook with regularity and I knew that he would read anything I posted. So I posted a thought about the logical results of parents just wanting their kids to be happy. My friend liked the post and I asked that God would give me an opportunity to engage him in person with that thought. The opportunity came the next day. I used the post as a gospel bridge and said, "I remember you telling me that you did not want to take your son to church unless he wanted to go. Isn't this the same philosophy of the parenting you believe is detrimental?" He saw the apparent contradiction. That led to me telling him the importance of regularly attending church. He brought his son several weeks later and eventually gave his heart to the Lord.

Much of exploring is simply asking the right questions. You need to think less about being interesting and more about being interested. Ask questions, listen, and be alert. If you are intentional about your conversations with the people on your name list, then you will soon get to engage them on a spiritual level.

Take a look at your name list. What can you do this week to move a person from surface talk to personal talk?

_____

_____

_____

Stimulate

When exploring has gone on too long, you will need to stimulate their interest. Contrary to popular belief, most of the lost people on your name list are not hostile atheists. More than likely they are in one of two categories: A "none" or a deceived unbeliever. A "none" is a part of the fastest growing religious category in the United States. "Nones" are those who do not identify with any religious group. Their religion is nothing in particular.

Another group much harder to categorize is people who identify as Christian but are actually not true believers. According to Barna Research, seventy-three percent of Americans identify as Christians. If seventy-three percent of Americans were actually believers, we would have traffic on Sunday mornings. But, alas, the roads are far from congested. When a self-identified Christian attends a religious service at least once a month and says their faith is very important in their life, the numbers drop to around one in three U.S. adults (31%).[xix] According to the primary marks of a true believer found in First John, there are a significant number of people in our country that are placing their eternal hopes on a lie.

One group is apathetic and the other group is deceived. Sometimes the one thing both groups need is something to stimulate their curiosity. They need questions that will get them to seriously consider their standing before God. Alvin Reid suggests these questions to stimulate further consideration of spiritual matters:

- If you ever want to talk about the difference between religion and Christianity, let me know.
- When you attend church, where do you attend?
- Have you thought more lately about spiritual things?
- Would you say you have a personal relationship with Jesus Christ, or are you still in the process?
- In your opinion, what is a real Christian?
- What do you think of _____? (God, Jesus, the Bible)
- Who do you think Jesus Christ was?
- We've been friends for a while. Could I share with you a very important part of my life?[xx]

These stimulating questions can be used whether you have been working on a friendship for months or if you are talking with them for the first time. On occasion you will encounter situations where you know you will probably never see the person again. Whether you are on vacation, in a taxi, getting a haircut, or on a mission trip, sometimes it is "now or never." Bill Hybels suggests these questions to quickly get to spiritual matters:

- I'm curious, do you ever think about spiritual matters?
- Who in your opinion was Jesus Christ?
- What's your spiritual background? Were you taught a particular religious perspective as you grew up?
- Do you ever wonder what happens to us when we die?
- What do you think a real Christian is?
- Where are you heading in your spiritual journey?[xxi]

Again, these questions are most often used when "exploring" has run dry. You have established trust. You demonstrated that you care for them. But you are struggling to take it to the next level. If so, perhaps it is time to use the more direct method and stimulate a spiritual conversation. You will be amazed how these simple questions can begin a process that will ultimately revolutionize the life of the other person.

Who on your name list has been in the "personal level" for a long time but needs to be stimulated to take them to the "spiritual level?"

_____

_____

_____

Share

The best and most effective way to transition a friendship to a spiritual level is by sharing your story. It is often called your testimony. No one can deny your experience. If you are a Christian, your story includes a time when you were lost and following your own path. You then became aware of the good news of Jesus Christ and either readily accepted the free gift or spent a season battling with God. At some point you finally surrendered your life to Christ and happily received salvation by grace through faith.

The details of your story are as unique and varied as a snowflake. Every story is different. Some are more dramatic than others. But a high level of drama is not a prerequisite to sharing. Every story is valid and worth sharing.

A person can argue the facts of the Bible all day long, but they cannot discredit your story. Using your story as a gospel bridge is effective because you immediately become relatable. Everyone has a story. Your pre-Christ story is particularly relatable because it is going to have similarities to their story.

In fact, they may be surprised to find out that you were not born a Christian. So many people view Christianity like a last name, as though it is something you inherit when you enter the world. Parents from a Jewish or Muslim background do not look to convert their children because they believe their children are already born into the religion. Obviously this is not the case with Christianity. We are born sinners and need to believe the gospel before becoming a Christian.

Your testimony has three parts: your life before Christ, your awareness of the truths of the gospel, and your actual conversion. Each part is unique and important to the overall story. As we look at each part, we will see how Paul used his testimony to build a bridge to the gospel in Acts 26:9-18.

Life Before Christ

It may feel like a lifetime ago, but you did have a time in your life before you were a Christian. Since the majority of Christians were converted during childhood, your recollection of life before Christ may be small. But do not skimp on this part just because you may have been young.

I was saved when I was eleven years old. By all accounts I was a pretty good kid. I did not get into any major trouble and was generally kind to people. Never the less, my heart was not toward God. If a machine could read thoughts, I would never want anyone to read the results. My daily motives often revolved around what I wanted. I was very good at hiding my darkened heart with a big smile, some good manners, and pleasant personality. Though my sinful life before Christ was not dramatic by any stretch of the imagination, the depths of my depravity cannot by evaluated by the level of drama. On a daily basis I ruled my kingdom though Christ was knocking on the door of my heart.

Paul's life before Christ was much different. In Acts 26, starting in verse four, Paul described the "manner of life from [his] youth." He said, "I myself was convinced that I ought to do many things in opposing the name of Jesus of Nazareth. And I did so in Jerusalem. I not only locked up many of the saints in prison after receiving authority from the chief priests, but when they were put to death I cast my vote against them. And I punished them often in all the synagogues and tried to make them blaspheme, and in raging fury against them I persecuted them even to foreign cities" (Acts 26:9-11).

If Paul were alive today we would have called him a former religious terrorist. His life before Christ was not much different than those Islamic terrorists that are blinded by their raging fury to do what they think is pleasing to God. Paul's life before Christ was more dramatic than my story, but I can relate because I, too, was pursuing a life of selfish ambition. I too was all about myself, often at the expense of others. I was just more discreet about my sins.

If Paul were alive today we would have called him a former religious terrorist.

As you think about articulating your own life before Christ, do not glorify that time. I have heard many testimonies that go something like this: "I was the life of the party. I could outlast everyone. My name is on the wall of the bar for my drinking prowess. Everyone loved me." Sometimes we are tempted to embellish the story in order to make it more interesting. You can accidentally come across as making your past sound more appealing than your new life in Christ. Just tell the truth about your life before Christ with a sense of gratefulness that God delivered you from it.

Begin to put together an outline of your life before Christ. How would you characterize your life before grace, forgiveness, and hope?

_____

_____

_____

Awareness of the Gospel

At some point along your journey you became aware of the truths of the gospel. On average, a person hears the gospel five or six times before they come to faith. You probably spent some time thinking through these startling claims. What was that like? In my own story, my mother and father sent me to a private Christian school where I learned the truth, sang songs about Jesus, and saw Christianity lived out in the lives of my teachers.

Paul's conversion story continues to be dramatic. I suppose it had to be considering the life he was leading. Paul describes part two of his testimony in Acts 26:12-18, "In this connection I journeyed to Damascus with the authority and commission of the chief priests. At midday, O king, I saw on the way a light from heaven, brighter than the sun, that shone around me and those who journeyed with me. And when we had all fallen to the ground, I heard a voice saying to me in the Hebrew language, 'Saul, Saul, why are you persecuting me? It is hard for you to kick against the goads.' And I said, 'Who are you, Lord?' And the Lord said, 'I am Jesus whom you are persecuting. But rise and stand upon your feet, for I have appeared to you for this purpose, to appoint you as a servant and witness to the things in which you have seen me and to those in which I will appear to you, delivering you from your people and from the Gentiles—to whom I am sending you to open their eyes, so that they may turn from darkness to light and from the power of Satan to God, that they may receive forgiveness of sins and a place among those who are sanctified by faith in me."

Paul was struck with blindness and personally heard Jesus calling out to him. This is an exceptional story and probably not like yours. But do not discount the importance of wrestling with the gospel truth claims. It is part of the conversion process. Jesus said, "Whoever does not bear his own cross and come after me cannot be my disciple" (Luke 14:27). Paul had to renounce everything he had ever believed to be true. He had to join with those whom he had vehemently hated and persecuted.

What about you? Did you count the cost as you became aware of the gospel? What was the process like? Was the gospel like water to a parched mouth or did you wrestle with God for a while?

Put into writing how you heard the gospel? Did you readily respond or did it take you a while?

_____

_____

_____

Conversion

In some theological circles good people debate whether or not conversion happens over time or is encapsulated with a specific time and place. Indeed many Christians struggle to identify a precise time when they became a Christian. However the Bible points to a number of very significant changes upon conversion:

- We are forgiven (Luke 7:48)
- We are adopted into the family of God (Galatians 4:5)
- We get Heavenly citizenship (Ephesians 2:19)
- We become a new creature (2 Corinthians 5:17)
- We are reconciled to God (Romans 5:10)
- We have our name recorded in the Book of Life in heaven (Luke 10:20)
- We are sealed by the Holy Spirit (Ephesians 1:13)
- We are indwelt by the Holy Spirit (Romans 8:11)

The Bible does not have any verses suggesting there is a time when we are partially adopted in the family or mostly reconciled to God. You will not find anything suggesting your name written in pencil in the book

66

of life or only moderately sealed by the Holy Spirit. The reality is that if you are a Christian, at some point in your life you moved from darkness to light. You had your sins fully forgiven and are now on a path toward eternity with God. How amazing is that?

My moment came on a hot July night at Camp Zephyr in the middle of south Texas. The camp preacher had been boldly proclaiming the gospel night after night. He did not say anything that I did not already know. But God set forth that time for me to surrender my life to the Lord. A deep sense of guilt overwhelmed me along with the amazement Jesus Christ would go to the cross for one such as me. That night in the "Tabernacle" of Zephyr Baptist Encampment, long after my friends had left the building and were catching fireflies, I received the free gift of salvation by placing my faith in my Lord Jesus.

In Paul's testimony before King Agrippa he simply said, "I was not disobedient to the heavenly vision" (Acts 26:19). In other words, he did, exactly what Jesus told him to do. Paul verified his claim by saying he went to Damascus, Jerusalem, and all the regions of Judea to let the world know he was now a Christian. Do you remember when you stepped across the line and became a Christian?

In a few words, can you recount the day and time you placed your faith in Jesus?

_____

_____

_____

Next Step

Now you can start putting your entire testimony together. Again, the first part is about your life before Christ. It should be different than your life as a new creature in Christ! Next is your growing awareness of the truths of the gospel. Most people hear the gospel five or six times before placing their faith in Christ. What was that process like for you? Finally your testimony includes your conversion experience. What were the circumstances around the day and time you "officially" placed your faith in Jesus?

Some people add a fourth part to their story. Your walk with Christ as a believer is also a significant part of who you are. Jesus has carried you through some dark and difficult times. You know that you would be in a world of trouble were it not for the grace and mercy of God. Feel free to add this important part to your testimony. Grab a notebook and take some time writing out your testimony. Get familiar with it so that you will be ready to build a bridge to the gospel.

Chapter Seven
How to Share the Gospel on a Napkin

Yesterday I got to share the gospel with a young lady. Recently her boyfriend came into my office because he was at the end of his running from God. The Lord graciously chose me to be the one to lead him to faith in Jesus. As he left my office I told him to tell all his friends about what happened. Naturally he told his girlfriend who had already seen something different about him. Later that week I got a message from the young man that his girlfriend wanted to talk with me about "taking the same path."

As I drove to speak to them, an illogical fear began to creep in. What if I say the wrong thing? Never mind that I thoroughly know the gospel story. Disregard that I have been in full-time church ministry for sixteen years. Ignore the fact that I have a Master of Divinity and Doctor of Ministry degrees. I was nervous and even concerned about saying the wrong thing.

Gospel encounters rarely go the way that you imagine. Due to some issues with the location we had to move our meeting to a coffee shop. We all got our beverages and sat at a table outside. The young lady was very open to the gospel. God gave me the exact words she needed to hear. The Holy Spirit was clearly at work. God's Word cut to her heart like a two-edged sword. She surrendered her life to the Lord.

As I drove away and was thanking God for using me in that way, I had to chuckle. Why was I nervous about saying the wrong thing? God is in control and will use even my incoherent, garbled words to reach a person for Christ. But even though that is the case, I was ready, willing, and able to articulate the gospel. In chapter two you were encouraged to be ready and willing to share the gospel to anyone, at anytime, and anywhere. But are you able? Can you actually share the gospel if you had one minute, five minutes, or as much time as you need? This chapter will help you be prepared when that opportunity arises.

The Apostle Peter said, "But in your hearts revere Christ as Lord. Always be prepared to give an answer to everyone who asks you to give the reason for the hope that you have" (1 Peter 3:15 NIV). We are called to "always be prepared." In chapter two I emphasized the "always." But as much as we are called to be ready to share, we are also called to be "prepared to give an answer." You should know what you believe, why you believe it, and be able to explain what you believe to someone else. You are called to be ready at a moment's notice to share the gospel.

The gospel has been encapsulated into dozens of acronyms, alliterations, imagery, similes, and metaphors. While each have their merit and are effective in their own ways, I have found the current postmodern culture – especially young adults, teenagers, and children – responds best to the gospel in story form.

The gospel starts with God in the beginning. It unfolds through the fall of man into sin and the rescue through Jesus. It culminates in the future with the new heavens and the new earth. Creation, fall, redemption, and restoration are not only God's plan but are also His story. God commissioned us to become master storytellers through evangelism.

You are going to learn how to communicate this story and simply draw it out. If you have the opportunity to share the gospel at a restaurant or coffee shop, you can grab a napkin and draw out the story in four simple chapters.

Chapter One: In the Beginning...God

The story begins with God. In fact, it is all about God. Contrary to popular psychology, the world does not revolve around you. This is God's story and you are a wonderful part of it. This first chapter includes answers to questions such as, "Where did I come from?" and "Why am I here?" But it fundamentally begins with God as Creator.

The Bible begins, "In the beginning, God created the heavens and the earth" (Genesis 1:1). The Bible wastes no time in introducing the main character of history. But God is not just a clockmaker that sets the parts in motion then leaves it alone. He saved humans as His last and seminal creation. He put Adam and Eve in charge of the earth and gave them everything they needed in life.

Above all else in the creation account we see that God wanted to have a relationship with His human creation. He looked at all He had made and declared it good. The earth only had a vague resemblance to what we see today. In the beginning the earth was in harmony. Adam and Eve lived fluidly with the animals. The ground produced all the food they could need. They had each other for companionship and they lived in perfect communion with God. All was right in the world.

In order to visually share this part of the story, I recommend drawing a picture of the earth. Do not get too detailed. A simple circle with a few squiggly lines in the middle will suffice. Write "In the beginning – God" underneath the drawing. I can emphasize enough that this is God's story of redemption. God is the central character. It is His love and compassion that compelled Him to send His only begotten Son not "to condemn the world, but in order that the world might be saved through him" (John 3:17).

The main points for you to remember in chapter one are:

1. God is the Creator.
2. He declared His creation as good.
3. Humans are his prized possession.

The main verse to memorize in chapter one is Genesis 1:1, which says, "In the beginning, God created the heavens and the earth." Before you proceed to the next chapter, stop and try to recite the story from memory. Imagine you are actually speaking to someone. Begin by saying, "It all starts with God. The Bible begins…"

Chapter Two: Sin

Whereas chapter one of the gospel story was ideal, the scenario quickly shifts in chapter two. Adam and Eve were made differently than all other creatures. At one time many scholars said humans were differentiated from animals because of our ability to use tools and to sophistically communicate. But we know now that some animals make and use tools as well. Other animals have complex methods of communication. The primary distinction between humans and all other animals is the spiritual component. We have a moral compass given to us by God. Animals are not responsible for their choices. My dog – who is as wonderful and loving as you can imagine – is not going to answer to God for the mess that he makes. But God communicates with us and has given us moral boundaries.

On a side note, it may be worth dispelling the notion that God is the big principal in the sky ready to use a paddle on us all. Many people see God as harsh and strict. It can come from personal experiences with an overbearing and unloving father. God does give us moral boundaries. Some people call those rules, laws, or commandments. But they are given to us out of a heart of love. God created us, loves us, and knows us intimately. He knows what is for our best. So rather than view the Bible's commands as strict, a better perspective is to view them as loving guides to help us experience the abundant life.

God commanded Adam and Eve to not eat the fruit from a specific tree. They chose to disobey God and introduced sin into the world. The sin of Adam and Eve was not simply eating an apple. They were guilty of believing they know better than God. They rebelled against God and fundamentally decided that they were smarter than their creator.

Sometimes one small act can have great consequences. Have you ever set up a long line of dominoes? When the first one is knocked over, it hits the second, and the second one hits the third, and the third hits the fourth. This chain reaction continues until every domino in the line falls. This chain reaction is called "the domino effect." The first domino does not fall in isolation. It brings others down with it. The first man was not the only one to fall. Adam brought down others. Adam's sin did not merely result in a fallen man; it resulted in a fallen race. All humans are fallen (including you and me). The Bible says, "for all have sinned and fall short of the glory of God" (Romans 3:23). The effects of sin can be seen everywhere.

Sin spreads like a fast moving virus. Adam and Eve's firstborn son murdered his brother. In the days of Noah, "the wickedness of man was great in the earth, and that every intention of the thoughts of his heart was only evil continually" (Genesis 6:5). In the days of Abraham the men were described as "wicked, great sinners against the Lord" (Genesis 13:13). In the days of Jesus, the people condemned and crucified the only man who had never sinned a day of his life!

Today we continue to see the dominoes fall. Despite some amazing advancements, especially in the areas of science, technology, and medicine, mankind is still exceptionally proficient at sinning. I would suggest that the advancements in knowledge have only puffed up the arrogance of God's precious creatures. We are still no different than Adam and Eve.

The biggest consequence of sin is death. The Bible says, "Therefore, just as sin came into the world through one man, and death through sin, and so death spread to all men because all sinned" (Romans 5:12). Sin brought death into the world. Not only did it introduce physical death, it killed the precious communion God desires with His people. Apart from an intervention, all people predictably choose to go their own path.

For chapter two of God's Story I recommend drawing a picture of a broken earth. This will be the most difficult of the drawings, but should not throw you off. See the picture on this page as an example. Write "Sin Destroys" underneath the drawing.

The main points for you to remember in chapter two are:

1. God gave us the ability to choose right and wrong.
2. When we choose to defy God, we sin.
3. Sin kills our relationship with God.

The main verse to memorize in chapter two is Romans 3:23 which says, "for all have sinned and fall short of the glory of God." Although no one likes to talk about sin – and some do not even like to use that word – it is a major part of the story. Without the problem of sin we cannot have the incredibly good news of salvation through Jesus Christ. If we hold back on addressing sin, the good news simply becomes acceptable news.

Chapter Three: Jesus

God thoroughly hates sin and the ravaging effects it has had upon all those whom He has created in His own image. The Bible says, "The Lord is not slow to fulfill his promise as some count slowness, but is patient toward you, not wishing that any should perish, but that all should reach repentance" (2 Peter 3:9). God does not desire that any would live and die apart from Him. He wants all to come to repentance and a restored relationship with Him.

At the very center of His being, God is love. He loves us as Creator. He loves us as Provider. He loves us as a good Father and compassionate Counselor. But His love is best expressed through giving us His only begotten Son. Certainly John 3:16 is a famous and familiar verse to point out His love, but I would also look to Romans 5:8 which says, "but God shows his love for us in that while we were still sinners, Christ died for us." God shows us His love by sending Jesus to die for us.

Why does Jesus have to die for us? Our sin has killed our relationship with God. We cannot restore it by paying God back because our sins are too numerous. If a thirty year old sinned only three times per day, Satan can bring up nearly eleven thousand instances of breaking God's law. Who could atone for so many crimes? All of humanity must plead guilty and be at the mercy of the Judge.

A good judge delivers justice. God is like a good judge who cannot wink at a broken law – much less ten thousand broken laws. Rather, He must deliver a guilty judgment. But in what must be considered the greatest act ever conceived, God offered up His Son Jesus to take the punishment in our place. God offers the free gift of declaring you righteous before Him if you will simply receive it. The penalty has been paid for by Jesus' death on the cross. Like any other gift, we cannot earn it. We can only receive it.

The world is broken because of sin. Every person living and breathing on this planet has fallen short of a right relationship with God. But because of God's great love for us, He made a way to be reconciled to Him through Jesus. The Bible says, "if you confess with your mouth that Jesus is Lord and believe in your heart that God raised him from the dead, you will be saved" (Romans 10:9). You must declare yourself to be a follower of the Lord Jesus and believe with all your heart that Jesus rose again on the third day.

For chapter three of God's Story I recommend drawing a picture of a broken earth with the cross over the world. Jesus' death on the cross and resurrection are the only hope for this shattered world. Write "Jesus Saves" underneath the drawing.

The main points for you to remember in chapter three are:

1. God loves you and wants you reconciled with Him.
2. God sent His Son Jesus to die on the cross for you.
3. You must receive the free gift by faith.

In the previous chapters you were not asked to memorize more than one verse. However chapter three is the apex of God's story. It is the most important part and needs the greatest attention. I recommend that you memorize the part of 2 Peter 3:9 that says, "[God] is patient toward you, not wishing that any should perish, but that all should reach repentance." Then memorize Romans 5:8, which says, "but God shows his love for us in that while we were still sinners, Christ died for us."

Finally be able to recite Romans 10:9, which says, "if you confess with your mouth that Jesus is Lord and believe in your heart that God raised him from the dead, you will be saved."

Chapter Four: New Earth

The fourth and final chapter is perhaps the least familiar in the gospel narrative. God's story will come to a fulfillment and we need to be ready to share about the hope that we have. The good news of the gospel is not just that God provides salvation and reconciliation through Jesus, but that He also rewards us with eternal blessings.

In the beginning there was no suffering. God and man were in a right relationship. Man and animals coexisted peacefully. The earth's ground provided all that man needed for food. There were no violent storms or dangerous earthquakes. It was all "very good" (Genesis 1:31).

But sin entered the picture and set off a domino effect. Whereas once there was no suffering or death, now every human dies, every human suffers, animals are dangerous, rivers flood and destroy crops, wildfires scorch the earth, earthquakes destroy whole cities, tornadoes indiscriminately tear through homes, and cancer touches nearly four out of ten people. The broken world points us to the obvious reality that something is dreadfully wrong. The consequences of sin are severe and a big deal.

Midway through his letter to the Romans, Paul reflected on the current state of the world and the hope for a better world:

[18] For I consider that the sufferings of this present time are not worth comparing with the glory that is to be revealed to us. [19] For the creation waits with eager longing for the revealing of the sons of God. [20] For the creation was subjected to futility, not willingly, but because of him who subjected it, in hope [21] that the creation itself will be set free from its bondage to corruption and obtain the freedom of the glory of the children of God. [22] For we know that the whole creation has been groaning together in the pains of childbirth

until now. [23] And not only the creation, but we ourselves, who have the firstfruits of the Spirit, groan inwardly as we wait eagerly for adoption as sons, the redemption of our bodies. Romans 8:18-23

For now we groan, along with creation, at the devastation of sin. But the children of God and His creation will be "set free from its bondage to corruption" (Romans 8:21). God promises us that in the future we will be completely free from sin and that creation will be free from the devastating effects of sin.

In the final book of the Bible we get the clearest picture of our future. John describes his divine vision of the future: "Then I saw a new heaven and a new earth, for the first heaven and the first earth had passed away, and the sea was no more... He will wipe away every tear from their eyes, and death shall be no more, neither shall there be mourning, nor crying, nor pain anymore, for the former things have passed away" (Revelation 12:1,4). The earth will be restored to its original design and those who followed Jesus in faith will live eternally with God and without sin.

Paul says in Ephesians 2:7 that God made us alive together with Christ and raised us up with him "so that in the coming ages he might show the immeasurable riches of his grace in kindness toward us in Christ Jesus." Can you imagine a greater promise? In the ages to come, God is going to unleash the immeasurable riches of His grace upon us. Sam Storms captures the beauty of this promise saying, "Like waves incessantly crashing on the shore, one upon another, so the ages of eternity future will, in endless succession, echo the celebration of sinners saved by grace, all to the glory of God. There will not be in heaven a one-time momentary display of God's goodness, but an everlasting, ever-increasing infusion and impartation of divine kindness that intensifies with every passing moment."[xxii]

For chapter four of God's Story I recommend drawing a picture of the earth with the cross above it. Our future will involve a new heaven and a new earth with Jesus ruling the kingdom. Write "Renewed" underneath the drawing.

The main points for you to remember in chapter three are:

1. Jesus is going to make all things new again.
2. Our reward – made possible by Jesus – is eternal joy.

The main verse to memorize in chapter four is Revelation 21:4 which says, "He will wipe away every tear from their eyes, and death shall be no more, neither shall there be mourning, nor crying, nor pain anymore, for the former things have passed away."

Next Step

The goal is for you to be able to conversationally tell God's story. Fortunately a story format does not demand that you have a script memorized. You need to know the general flow of the story and the main ideas. Since God's Word is His tool to penetrate the heart, you need to memorize the verses. Make a goal to memorize one of the selected verses per week and describe its meaning within the context of the chapter. For instance, this week memorize Genesis 1:1.

As you recite the verse, describe what is happening in chapter one of God's story. You do not need to memorize the main points word-for-word, but you should be able to generally know the points. Before long you will be conversationally telling God's story chapter-by-chapter.

Chapter Eight
Closing the Deal

Please forgive the crude sound of the chapter title. Evangelism is not sales. You are not a snake oil salesman and are not trying to con anyone into being a Christian. However, you are offering a free gift. More than that, you highly desire that they receive this gift. You would not be satisfied with a good friendship if you knew that your friend was headed toward eternity apart from God. You would not want your neighbor to assume that he or she is going to heaven because you all are friends.

Penn Jillette, half of the magician duo Penn and Teller, and an outspoken atheist, does not understand Christians that do not share their faith. "I don't respect that at all. If you believe that there's a heaven and hell and people could be going to hell or not getting eternal life or whatever, and you think that it's not really worth telling them this because it would make it socially awkward, and atheists who think that people shouldn't proselytize -- 'Just leave me alone, keep your religion to yourself. How much do you have to hate somebody to not proselytize?" Jillette asked. "How much do you have to hate somebody to believe that everlasting life is possible and not tell them that? If I believed beyond a shadow of a doubt that a truck was coming at you and you didn't believe it, and that truck was bearing down on you, there's a certain point where I tackle you. And this is more important than that."[xxiii]

We need to be serious and urgent about evangelism. In reality we cannot escape because we are dealing with matters of eternity. Hell is a bad place and eternity is a long time. Not only do we need to fish for the lost, we also need to reel them in. We need to share the gospel and ask them to give their hearts and lives to Jesus. In short, we need to close the deal.

Popping the Question

Eventually you will come to the end of chapter four of the gospel story. You have finished explaining the basics of the gospel and now you want them to respond. This is where you transition from sharing the gospel to actually leading them to Christ. Bill Hybels says, "The goal is not merely to tell people about Christ. That's just the process we use to reach the goal, which is to lead people to Christ."[xxiv]

The New Testament records several actual witnessing encounters. They all conclude with a way to respond. In Acts 3, Peter concludes his sermon at Pentecost with a call to action, saying, "Repent and be baptized every one of you in the name of Jesus Christ for the forgiveness of your sins, and you will receive the gift of the Holy Spirit" (Acts 2:38). In the next chapter of Acts, Peter had attracted a crowd through healing a lame man. He used the opportunity to share the gospel. He concluded his presentation saying, "Repent therefore, and turn back, that your sins may be blotted out" (Acts 3:19). In the eighth chapter of Acts, Philip came upon a man who was simply ready to respond to whatever the Spirit was saying. Philip "told him the good news about Jesus" (Acts 8:35). The man was so excited that he pulled Philip to the first body of water he could find and asked to be baptized.

Luke records an instance when Paul and Silas were together in jail. Rather than sulking, the two men of God were "praying and singing hymns to God, and the prisoners were listening to them" (Acts 16:25). You can imagine that their prayers and songs were filled with gospel truths. Everyone within earshot was hearing the gospel proclaimed. Suddenly an earthquake rocked the city and caused the doors to the jail cells to open. The jailer's only job was to keep the prisoners in their cells. With the prisons now compromised, the jailer knew he might be punished with death. He went to Paul and said, "Sirs, what must I do to be saved?" (Acts 16:30). Paul responded, "Believe in the Lord Jesus, and you will be saved, you and your household" (Acts 16:31).

According to the above examples of evangelism, how would you ask a person to become a believer?

_____

_____

_____

There is not one specific way to call upon a person to give their life to Jesus. The modern evangelism presentations all offer different ways to ask the same question. Several popular examples are listed below.

Evangelism Explosion: The prospect is led to the question, "If you want to receive the gift of eternal life through Jesus Christ, then call on Him, asking Him for this gift right now."[xxv]

The Four Spiritual Laws: This popular gospel outline finishes with the appeal, "I invite you to pray this prayer right now, and Christ will come into your life, as He promised."[xxvi]

F.A.I.T.H.: After going through the acronym, the prospect is asked, "Understanding what we have shared, would you like to receive this forgiveness by trusting in Christ as your personal Savior and Lord?"[xxvii]

Steps to Peace With God: Billy Graham's gospel presentation used at many of his revivals asks, "Would you like to receive God's forgiveness?"[xxviii]

The Bridge Illustration: The creators of this gospel presentation ask a hypothetical question and then answer it. "So how can I have peace with God, life to the full, and be confident of eternal life like these verses say? First, through an honest prayer to God, I have to admit that I'm not perfect—that I can't escape my sins, and I can't save myself. I follow this admission by believing that Jesus Christ died for me on the cross and rose from the grave, conquering death and sin. Then I invite Jesus Christ to live in me and be the Lord of my life, accepting His free gift of eternal life with Him."[xxix]

Again there is not just one way to lead a person to Christ. Personally I like to ask, "Is there any reason why you would not receive this gift of eternal life through Jesus?" Hopefully the good news I just presented is so compelling that the person would have trouble coming up with a reason to not accept the gospel.

They Said Yes!

You have made it through the gospel story. You asked them if they want to believe in Jesus. They responded positively! What do you do now? This is extremely important because you want to help them make their first expression of faith. As a reminder, the Bible says, "if you confess with your mouth that Jesus is Lord and believe in your heart that God raised him from the dead, you will be saved" (Romans 10:9). The word confess means to verbally make known the inward conviction. To "confess with your mouth that Jesus is Lord" means to say "Yes! Yes, I believe. Yes, I will follow Jesus. Yes, I will turn from my own ways." Christians in the early church who would not deny Christ as their Lord were called "Confessors."[xxx]Therefore you will want to lead them to confess verbally that Jesus is Lord.

There are no magical words that get a person into heaven. One cannot simply say, "Jesus is Lord" and be assured of their eternal destiny. In fact, Jesus warned against it. He said, "Not everyone who says to me, 'Lord, Lord,' will enter the kingdom of heaven" (Matthew 7:21). Confession is verbally declaring an inward belief. The confession of Jesus as Lord means you are declaring allegiance to a new king. You are not simply saying you believe Jesus once lived. You are not even saying He was an amazing man who performed many miracles. It is much more than that. You are saying you surrender your life to a new ruler. Jesus is in charge now.

There are a variety of ways to lead a person to confess Jesus is Lord. The important principle to remember is that there is nothing magical in words. You cannot have them repeat a prayer and lead them to believe in some mystical phrases. I remember a coworker of mine many years ago asking me the words to "that prayer." When I finally figured out what he was talking about, I did an Internet search and emailed it to him. Unfortunately I missed a golden opportunity to explain the amazing gospel truths behind the words that I sent.

You have explained the gospel and they want the free gift of eternal life through Jesus. They might need help expressing their new faith in words. Sometimes leading them through a prayer of repentance and faith will help them confess Jesus as Lord. You may want to preface the prayer with saying, "These words do not save you. They are meant to be a reflection of your heart. So if you fully believe with all your heart these words, then repeat after me…

> Dear God, I know that I am a sinner. I have messed up and gone my own path. I am guilty of choosing my way over your way. I need forgiveness. Thank you for sending your son Jesus to die on the cross for me so that I may be forgiven. Thank you that He rose again on the third day to give me new life. I am yours now. Please help me follow you. In Jesus name I pray, amen!

Now celebrate! Give them a hug, a high five, or a handshake. Luke 15:10 says, "there is joy before the angels of God over one sinner who repents." This is an exciting time and your attitude should reflect it.

Describe a time when you saw someone come to faith in Christ. Was there excitement, tears, relief, etc.?

_____

_____

_____

You are Now a Spiritual Parent

You have a spiritual newborn on your hands. They are a baby in Christ and essentially brand new to Christianity. They have not learned the "basic principles of the oracles of God" (Hebrews 5:12). Just like a real newborn, they need help. They need a spiritual mother or father to guide, protect, and nurture them. Below you will find several essential steps you can take right away to help them navigate their new life in Christ.

Before they leave your sight you need to encourage them to tell others about their decision. As they grow in Christ they will probably begin to disassociate with some of their friends and acquaintances that live lifestyles in opposition to God's commands. There is no better time to reach these people. Your spiritual child is motivated and excited about what just happened. Recently I led a young man to Christ in my office. As he left I told him to tell all his friends what had happened. Two days later I got a message on my phone saying his girlfriend wanted to go down the same path. By God's grace I had two new spiritual children within a week!

The Bible points to baptism as the first priority after becoming a new believer. However, how can a new believer know this important truth unless you tell them? We encourage baptism to happen shortly after their conversion experience because it is a public declaration that they are not ashamed to be a new believer. Baptism is also an opportunity to demonstrate obedience to the Lord. As their spiritual parent you can teach them that baptism symbolizes a death to their old way of living and a commitment to living out a new life in Christ. Lead them to the baptismal waters as soon as possible.

Many new believers will already know that church attendance is normal for Christians. However the church has an image problem in the world of nonbelievers. Your new brother or sister in Christ just came from the world and may be very hesitant about attending – especially if he or she has tattoos, is a single parent, does not own any "church clothes," or thinks the preacher is going to rain down judgment on them.

But their participation in a local, Bible-believing church is absolutely critical. Greg Laurie says, "Jesus only started one organization when He walked this earth, and that was the church. Jesus loves the church, and so should we."[xxxi] If your new convert questions the importance of attending church, you can give them these reasons:

1. God said it is important. This is not just your opinion. God's Word warns against "not neglecting to meet together, as is the habit of some" (Hebrews 10:25). This is a matter of trusting that God knows best.

2. Worshipping Jesus together is powerful. There is power in numbers, and that certainly is the case with the church. There is an indescribable force when the church worships God in unity.

3. We grow more together. Spiritual growth is limited in isolation. But it is limitless when we "stir up one another to love and good works" (Hebrews 10:24).

4. We can accomplish more together. When the church comes together for a mission, it can build more homes, feed more mouths, clothe more people, and care for more orphans and widows.

Fortunately you are not alone in helping lead your spiritual child in their new life in Christ. Small groups within the context of the local church are places where new believers should flourish. Many small groups have the reputation of being inward focused and apathetic to visitors. May it never be! The first small groups found in Acts 2 were very tight, but the Lord "added to their number day by day those who were being saved" (Acts 2:47). Clearly God wants new believers to be welcomed into small groups and brought into their disciple-making culture. Lead them to a small group in the church.

Your new brother or sister in Christ needs you to teach them a few of the basic spiritual disciplines such as prayer and Bible reading. You want them to ultimately be able to feed themselves. One of the major milestones of moving from a toddler to a child is the ability to grab a fork or a spoon and put food in your mouth. You do not want to create an unhealthy dependence upon you. Teach them the basics of talking with

God and reading the Bible on a regular basis. Launch them into spiritual growth through these basic Christian disciplines.

Finally, expect to provide long term spiritual nurturing. You were granted a tremendous privilege to lead them to faith in Christ. Now you get to be their spiritual parent. You get to help them grow up in Christ. The Christian life is said to progress from infancy to childhood to adolescence and then to full maturity. Just like in life, each stage has particular needs. The infant needs protection and a high level of guidance. But as they grow, they become less dependent and able to express their unique gifts and talents. My daughter is nine years old and beginning to grow in maturity. For instance, we have transitioned from me telling her what the Bible says to me asking her what she thinks it says. Before long she will be really applying the Bible to her every day life. In the same way, you need to take a degree of ownership in their spiritual progress.

You have loved your friend, neighbor, coworker, or family member so much that you took a risk and pointed them to Christ. Now that you have led them to new life in Christ, you are their spiritual parent. Although this is not a formal title, it is now your joy to see them experience the abundant life in Christ. In summary, you ought to take the following steps:

1. Implore them to immediately tell their friends about what happened.
2. Lead them to the baptismal waters.
3. Invite them to church and help them see the importance of weekly attendance.
4. Get them plugged into a small group that will welcome them and help them grow in Christ.
5. Teach them a couple of the basic Christians disciplines such as prayer and Bible reading.
6. Expect to provide long term spiritual nurturing. You are not meant to guide them everywhere and all the time. But be their mentor and friend through the years.

The Time to Start is Now

You are not going to reach everyone for Christ. But you can reach some. There is absolutely nothing like being used by God to lead another person to faith in Christ. The feeling of joy is indescribable.

Perhaps you have read through this book and not yet taken any real steps toward leading someone to Christ. The time to start is now. You are very capable. No one is more suited to reach your friends, neighbors, coworkers, and family members than you. Do not let Satan trick you into thinking you are incompetent or unqualified.

Remember, God takes the pressure off because He does the saving. The Holy Spirit is actively working both in their life and in your life. He will give you the words to say. The Bible is your tool to reach them at a heart-level. God is just waiting on you to act in faith and obedience. Are you ready?

Get your name list and pray daily for them. Ask your Christian friends to join you in praying for these people. Make plans to transition your interaction with them from surface-level to personal. This will later give you a bridge to move on to a spiritual level. You are well on your way to bringing them to faith in Christ!

May God bless you every step of the way. May He give you the right people to pursue. May God give you a heart of compassion for the lost. May the Lord grant you much favor in your journey. May God use you to bring someone to faith in Jesus Christ!

[i] Murray J. Harris, *The Second Epistle to the Corinthians: a Commentary On the Greek Text* (Grand Rapids, Mich.: Paternoster & Wm B Eerdmans, 2005), 445.

[ii] Greg Laurie, *Tell Someone: You Can Share the Good News* (Nashville: B&H Books, 2016), 14.

[iii] "A Matthew Is Not a Statistic!." *My Hope with Billy Graham* (blog), January 2, 2013. http://www.myhopewithbillygraham.org.uk/not_a_statistic/.

[iv] According to the research done by Avner Ben-Ner, Brian P. McCall, Massoud Stephane, and Hua Wang in their paper "Identity and Self-Other Differentiation in Work and Giving Behaviors: Experimental Evidence"

[v] Michael Frost, *Surprise the World: the Five Habits of Highly Missional People* (Colorado Springs, CO: NavPress, 2015), 1.

[vi] God's Word Translation

[vii] for more information see www.hisbridgebuilders.org

[viii] Adapted from Bill Hybels's *Becoming a Contagious Christian.*

[ix] https://www.instagram.com/thinkgrowprosper/

[x] https://etymology.quora.com/Salary-Salt-Money

[xi] http://www.offthegridnews.com/off-grid-foods/how-long-will-it-keep-preserving-meat/

[xii] John R.W. Stott, *The Message of the Sermon On the Mount (Matthew 5-7): Christian Counter-Culture*(Leicester: IVP Academic, 1985), 34.

[xiii] The Survey of Construction conducted by the U.S. Census Bureau shows that the size of new construction has increased over the years. See http://www.census.gov/const/www/charindex.html for additional information.

[xiv] Bill Hybels and Mark Mittelberg, *Becoming a Contagious Christian*, Revised ed. (Grand Rapids, MI: Zondervan, 1996), 98.

[xv] http://www.desiringgod.org/articles/six-lessons-in-good-listening

[xvi] According to biblegateway.com, one of the leading online Bible resources

xvii http://www.globalgolfpost.com/now/2016/09/26/top-10-palmer-quotes

xviii Alvin Reid, *Evangelism Handbook: Biblical, Spiritual, Intentional, Missional* (Nashville, TN: B&H Academic, 2009), 257.

xix https://www.barna.com/research/state-church-2016/

xx Reid, 257-258.

xxi Hybels and Mittelberg, 139-140.

xxii http://samstorms.com/enjoying-god-blog/post/ever-increasing-grace

xxiii http://www.bpnews.net/29863/atheism-penn-jillette-ur-gesevangelism

xxiv Hybels and Mittelberg, 183.

xxv http://evangelismexplosion.org/resources/steps-to-life/step-7-commitment/

xxvi http://crustore.org/fourlawseng.htm

xxvii http://www.wbcjax.com/FAITH

xxviii https://peacewithgod.net

xxix https://www.navigators.org/Tools/Evangelism%20Resources/Tools/The%20Bridge%20to%20Life

xxx http://earlychurch.com/donatists.php

xxxi Laurie, 112.